The Big Book of
Personality
Tests for
Women

The Big Book of Personality Tests for Women

100 Fun-to-Take, Easy-to-Score Quizzes That Reveal Your Hidden Potential in Life, Love, and Work

Robin Westen

ISBN-13: 978-1-57912-781-7

Library of Congress Cataloging-in-Publication Data
Westen, Robin
The big book of personality tests for women: 100 fun-to-take, easy to score quizzes that reveal your hidden potential in life, love, and work / Robin Westen.
p. cm.
Includes bibliographical references and index.
ISBN 978-1-57912-781-7 (alk. paper)
1. Women—Psychology. 2. Questions and answers. I. Title.
HQ1206.W46 2008
155.6'33—dc22

Cover design: Liz Driesbach
Interior design: Liz Trovato

Manufactured in China

Published by
Black Dog & Leventhal Publishers, Inc.
151 West 19th Street
New York, NY 10011

Distributed by
Workman Publishing Company
225 Varick Street
New York, NY 10014

g f e d c b a

For my father, Morris Westen, the Answer Man

Contents

Part Two
Your Relationships

Part Three
Your Career

Introduction

Few of us would argue with the philosopher Socrates, who said, "An unexamined life is not worth living." But what tools should we use to dig deeper and uncover our true selves? Do we need years of costly psychoanalysis or monthlong solitary retreats on a meditation cushion—or is there a faster, easier, less expensive, and much more enjoyable way to discover our inner truths?

Years ago, if anyone claimed personality traits could be revealed by people's choice of music, the kind of ice-cream topping they preferred, their morning routine, the way they slept in bed or parted their hair, I probably would have been, at the very least, dubious. More likely, I'd have been bent over in knee-slapping laughter.

Well, today I don't think it's so funny.

After writing almost a thousand personality quizzes, interviewing hundreds of psychologists, doctors, professors, sociologists, researchers, and other leading experts in their fields, as well as reading through stacks of scientific studies—I know better. The fact is, every choice we make, from the way we come to our decisions, cope with difficulty, or exercise willpower to how we choose our friends or relieve stress, reveals hidden aspects of our true personalities. The keys are numerous: find them and the door to our unconscious swings open—if not to reveal every dark corner of our psyche, then at least to give a glimpse into the light.

In fact, by taking the quizzes in this book, you can discover a gamut of interesting insights about yourself: how flexible you really are, whether you can work from home, your parenting style, if you're ready for a change, whether you're open for romance; you can even measure your worldliness or find out what color fuels your passion. You can uncover the best time of day for you, why you're such a great host, or whether you need more solitary time or a pat on the back. Dozens of nuggets of self-knowledge can be yours just by answering some simple questions.

These short tests are the ideal way for busy yet curious women like you to discover hidden aspects within your personality, identify what really makes you tick, and get quick tips or even long-range strategies for tweaking your attitude, changing your behavior, and ultimately becoming happier and more satisfied with your life. Plus—they're fun!

Each test takes between one and ten minutes to complete; the scoring is always a snap and the analysis is practical and easy to comprehend. Often, the analysis includes helpful, step-by-step techniques and advice from leading experts.

The Big Book of Personality Tests for Women is divided into three sections: "Inner Life," "Relationships," and "Career." You can choose to focus on the area that most concerns you, or dip into each of them. Although the tests can be taken quickly, it's best to approach them with a clear mind and no distractions. In selecting your answers, go with your gut and trust your initial response. Studies show that most of the time, your first choice is on target and certainly the most revealing. For the best results, be completely honest in your answers. It's your choice whether you want to share the knowledge you gain with others, or keep it to yourself.

You might want to keep a sheet of paper and a pen or pencil nearby to write down your own conclusions about the issues each test raises and what your score reveals about you. It's a great way to reflect on your concerns—and to think about changes you might want to make in your life as a result of what you've learned.

Most important, relax and enjoy yourself. Remember: there are no right or wrong answers—only truthful ones.

Part One

Your Inner Life

1. How worldly are you?

Worldliness is something most of us think we possess, but it's not easy to define. It's not just a reflection of sophistication or the accumulation of frequent flyer miles, nor is it solely a matter of tolerance or flexibility. It's really about empathy—the capacity to see the world from another person's point of view and accept that view without judgment. It's an especially important trait in today's world, when the clash of cultures is often felt not only on a physical level—because of the sheer proximity of people—but on a psychological level as well. As the planet gets smaller, worldliness becomes essential for peaceful and harmonious living. And while it may be easy to point the finger at others and criticize their narrow view, it's not so easy to pin it down in ourselves.

If you take this quiz honestly, you will discover where you fall within the bigger picture. And it will help guide you toward broadening your outlook, if necessary.

1. **You think that:**

   a. Censorship is necessary to preserve moral standards.

   b. A small degree of censorship may be necessary, to protect children, for instance.

   c. All censorship is wrong.

2. **If you were traveling abroad and found that conditions were much less hygienic than you are used to, you would:**

   a. Probably adapt quite easily

   b. Laugh at your own discomfort

   c. Try to check into a five-star hotel ASAP

3. **Do you ever read a periodical which supports political views different from your own?**

   a. Never.

   b. Sometimes, if I come across one.

   c. Yes, I make a special effort to read them.

4. **When you read fiction, you:**

   a. Prefer to read about people much like yourself

   b. Prefer to read about people very different from you

   c. Enjoy escaping into a world where the incidents are more important than the characters

5. **Which statement do you most agree with?**

   a. A better society would reduce the need for crime.

   b. If crime were more severely punished, there would be less of it.

   c. I wish I knew the answer to the problem of crime.

6. **If you adhere to a particular religion, do you think that:**

   a. All religions have something to offer their believers.

b. Your religion is the only "right" one—although you're tolerant of others.

c. Nonbelievers are deficient in morality.

7. **Conversely (if you are not a religious believer), you think that:**

a. Only small-minded or stupid people are religious.

b. Religion can be a dangerous and evil force.

c. Religion seems to be good for some people.

8. **How many languages other than English do you speak—even minimally?**

a. Three or more

b. One or two

c. None

9. **Would you consider marrying someone of a different race?**

a. Yes.

b. No.

c. Not without thinking carefully about the various problems involved.

10. **Most of your friends are:**

a. People like you

b. Very different from you and from one another

c. Like you in some aspects, but different in others

11. **When you meet someone who disagrees with your views, you:**

a. Enjoy a good argument and keep your cool

b. Often argue and eventually lose your temper

c. Avoid the argument

12. **You think people who move to the United States should:**

a. Adapt completely to our culture

b. Honor their native beliefs and customs but learn English

c. Do whatever they choose to do

13. **Do you think it's possible to have a healthy long-distance love affair?**

a. Yes, thanks to e-mail. Besides, absence makes the heart grow fonder.

b. Personally, I wouldn't do it, but I suppose it works for some couples.

c. No. It's living in La-La Land.

14. **When a friend does something you very much disapprove of, you:**

a. Break the friendship. You would be a hypocrite not to.

b. Tell her how you feel, but keep in touch.

c. Tell yourself it's none of your business and behave toward her as you always have in the past.

15. **When you see someone with an extraordinary number of body piercings and tattoos, you feel:**

a. Uneasy

b. Curious

c. Disdainful

16. **You consider yourself a sexual:**

a. Maverick

b. Maven

c. Mouse

17. **If you were offered a job abroad, you would:**

a. Pack and go!

b. Carefully weigh the pros and cons

c. Probably turn it down. You prefer the familiar to the unknown.

18. **Can you retrieve your e-mail internationally?**

   a. You haven't tried to.

   b. No.

   c. Yes.

Your Score

Give yourself the following number of points for each answer:

1. a-0, b-3, c-5	10. a-0, b-5, c-3
2. a-5, b-3, c-0	11. a-5, b-3, c-0
3. a-0, b-3, c-5	12. a-0, b-3, c-5
4. a-0, b-3, c-5	13. a-3, b-5, c-0
5. a-3, b-0, c-5	14. a-0, b-5, c-3
6. a-5, b-3, c-0	15. a-3, b-5, c-0
7. a-0, b-3, c-5	16. a-5, b-3, c-0
8. a-5, b-3, c-0	17. a-5, b-3, c-0
9. a-5, b-0, c-3	18. a-0, b-3, c-5

IF YOU SCORED BETWEEN 75 AND 90 POINTS:
You have GLOBAL vision.

There is a famous Zen saying, "It is the same and at the same time it is not the same. It is different and it is not different." You understand the poignancy of these words because you have a natural capacity for acceptance. You look to the core of individuals and see similarity rather than difference. When you do observe cultural differences, you have the ability to adapt easily to them. This extraordinary tolerance, broad-mindedness, and sophistication may have been nurtured by global travel. Or, your innate worldliness may be the result of a naturally empathetic nature. However the seed was planted, continue to nurture its further growth. If everyone on earth thought and behaved as you do, the world would eventually become a freer, more peaceful place.

IF YOU SCORED BETWEEN 55 AND 89 POINTS:
You have PANORAMIC vision.

As technology has brought the people of the world closer together, you've embraced globalization. This sort of economic and cultural worldliness is your forte; you whiz around in cyberspace, support free trade, understand the power of global markets, travel widely, attempt to speak foreign phrases, and absolutely adore international cuisines. But, look a little deeper and your view may be somewhat narrower than it first appears. Although you're tolerant of all cultures, you haven't much personal, one-on-one experience with diversity. If at all possible, try living abroad for at least six months (shorter visits to foreign countries—even if you avoid tourist haunts—limit your vision). Try to begin looking beyond appearances. In other words, get personal with your global view and you'll see further and deeper.

IF YOU SCORED FEWER THAN 54 POINTS:
You have LIMITED vision.

It's much easier to have a wider outlook and to be tolerant when you don't hold firm beliefs. But when you cling to strong ideology, whether it's left- or right-leaning, it's hard to see and embrace the whole picture. Look through the questions again and note where you picked up low scores. Were these the questions where personal comfort was directly concerned? Where strong ideological beliefs were touched upon? Or, was it where technological advances or world travel were involved? Once you pinpoint your area of limited vision, you can expand your horizons. It's very likely that you count yourself, or your culture, as inhabiting the highest moral ground. If you can widen your experience of life and deepen your contact with other cultures, your tolerance temperature will probably come down and your worldly vision will improve.

2. Are you ready for a change?

Change isn't always easy, but without a little every now and then, life can be dull. "There are signals we all give off that indicate whether we're ready for a little spontaneity, want to make a bigger change, or if the status quo is working as is," explains Susan Jeffers, PhD, author of *Life Is Huge: Laughing, Loving, and Learning from It All!* This test will tell you whether you're ripe for change.

1. **When the alarm rings in the morning, you:**
   a. Roll over and grab a little more sleep
   b. Arise immediately, wondering what the day ahead will bring
   c. Snuggle under the covers, making a mental list of all you need to do

2. **Check out your high school yearbook. What about you has remained the same?**
   a. Hair, makeup—maybe even some of the clothes
   b. Confidence
   c. Smile

3. **How often do you travel—even for a mini weekend break?**
   a. Rarely
   b. At least once a year
   c. A few times a year

4. **When you go to your favorite neighborhood restaurant, you usually:**
   a. Choose your one favorite entrée
   b. Order the special of the night
   c. Alternate among three favorite dishes

5. **On most weekends you can be found:**
   a. Playing catch-up on errands, grocery shopping, and cleaning
   b. Relaxing
   c. Socializing with friends and family

6. **When was the last time you met and made plans with a new friend?**
   a. Too long ago to remember
   b. Within the last year
   c. Within the past six months

Does hair make the woman? Thirty percent of us think so, believing that just changing our hair style or color can make us happier!

7. **Of these, you're more likely to day-dream about:**

a. Having more time to yourself

b. Choosing a different career

c. Winning the lottery

8. **When you see a makeover on TV, your first reaction is:**

a. I wish it were me.

b. I wonder what they would do to me.

c. Wow, she looks great!

Your Score

MOSTLY A'S:

You're in need of a change.

One of the most recognizable signs that you could use a change is daydreaming—and you probably do plenty of it. Sure, you like your life as it is, but there's a part of you that's itching for things to be a little different. On the flip side, sudden changes make you very uncomfortable. "Stepping outside of your comfort zone has its rewards, too—and it doesn't have to mean drastic change," says Susan Jeffers. Start with small things, such as rearranging the furniture in your home. And to begin the process of growing more comfortable with change:

- Tell yourself, "I can handle it!" "Repeating this affirmation can give you a sense of fortitude to embrace whatever comes along," says Jeffers.

- Take a mini getaway. Traveling to new places—even just an hour's drive away—can give you a fresh perspective. "We're more open to new directions when we're in unfamiliar surroundings," says Jeffers.

MOSTLY B'S:

You're ready to experiment a little!

Happy with your family and friends, you still wouldn't mind changing a few other things, including your daily routine. And that makes you the perfect candidate for tapping into your spontaneous side. What's the easiest way to do it? Start small. Here's how:

- Give yourself a mini makeover. Try a new haircut, add something flashy to your wardrobe, or dab on a new scent.

- Be a kid again. Stroll through the crafts store and pick up the first thing that interests you. Finding an artistic hobby not only makes you feel more carefree, but people who enjoy hobbies rate higher on scales of life satisfaction.

MOSTLY C'S:

You live for change!

Whether it's trying a hot new fashion trend or considering a job change, you tend to jump in with both feet. But sometimes that means you don't make sure that what you try will make you happier. To zero in on a positive change that's sure to please:

- Rethink your daily to-do list, putting a star next to activities you least enjoy. That will help you focus on ways to minimize them.

- Make a new friend. Bringing new people into your life can help you see yourself in a new light and open you to the possibilities that bring the most pleasure.

3. How well do you deal with anger?

Humans are a dominating, dangerous bunch, the most dangerous beings on earth. We've reached this powerful place by skillfully (and often ruthlessly) combining the "big three": intellectual savvy, muscular might, and manual dexterity. Impressive characteristics, yes, but alone they won't guarantee our survival. That's why behind it all lays a dynamic force, one urging us to compete and conquer. But here's the rub: if this dynamo inside us is blocked or hampered, it responds by becoming stronger, not weaker. The end product of this amplification: anger. Anger encourages us to compete rather than withdraw. Common sense and civility are often flung to the wind when wrath takes over, or, as Will Rogers once said, "People who fly into a rage always make a bad landing." In truth, Rogers was only half right: it doesn't matter whether anger is expressed or repressed. If you don't have a handle on your hostility, it will hurt either you or someone else. According to Redford Williams, MD, director of Behavioral Medicine at the Medical Center of Duke University and coauthor of *Anger Kills*, about 25 percent of our adult population has levels of hostility high enough to be dangerous to their health. Since anger is a complex emotion, there are various ways it can manifest itself. This quiz explores several possibilities. It will help you determine how well you vent and offer specific techniques to help tame the fiery monster within. So take a deep breath…and begin.

1. **When viewing virtual violence on television or in the movies, you are usually:**

   a. Ambivalent. You appreciate the actor's performance but you don't feel personally involved.

   b. Trying to avert your eyes

   c. Getting a vicarious thrill

2. **After a couple of drinks, you:**

   a. Usually feel carefree and relaxed

   b. Become a little withdrawn and moody

   c. Make sarcastic (but truthful) remarks that might otherwise be unspoken

3. **On the whole, how do you think our society deals with criminals?**

   a. We're too soft.

   b. We're too harsh.

   c. We're not perfect, but, overall, justice prevails.

4. **Life is full of daily annoyances, from slow elevators to bumper-to-bumper traffic. As a rule they:**

   a. Get under your skin

   b. Roll off your back

   c. Temporarily rankle

5. **Someone cuts you off on the highway. You are likely to:**

   a. Take a deep breath and let it go

   b. Honk your horn or make a rude gesture

   c. Be grateful you weren't hit

6. **Do you suffer from any of these tension-induced ailments: headaches, insomnia, stomach discomfort, or high blood pressure?**

   a. Rarely

   b. Frequently

   c. Never

7. **You are ordering something by catalog over the phone. A recording instructs you to "wait for the next available customer service representative." You are likely to:**

a. Hang up and call back another time

b. Hold on while feeling the annoyance mount

c. Use the time to check your e-mail

8. **Which statement is most true for you?**

a. I often get angry, even over small things. Plus, even when I know I'm wrong I find it hard to apologize.

b. It takes a lot to make me angry and when I blow up I feel a bit ashamed of myself.

c. I never lose my temper. I may feel angry, but I stay in control.

9. **If your partner was unfaithful, you would probably:**

a. Be angriest at the third party

b. Make your partner feel guilty and miserable

c. Blame yourself

10. **Your best friend is angry at you, but you don't think you deserve her ire. You are most likely to:**

a. Apologize anyway. It's not worth the ill will.

b. Talk it over and try to get her to see the other side

c. Just chill and wait for it to blow over

11. **Do you believe anger destroys love?**

a. Without a doubt.

b. Expressing all emotions can help a relationship.

c. Not necessarily, but it can certainly damage it.

12. **If you've had a rough day at work, are you likely to take it out on the people closest to you?**

a. Doesn't everybody?

b. Probably a little too often

c. Rarely, if ever

Your Score

Give yourself the following number of points for each answer:

1. a-5, b-3, c-0	7. a-3, b-0, c-5
2. a-5, b-3, c-0	8. a-0, b-5, c-3
3. a-0, b-5, c-3	9. a-0, b-5, c-3
4. a-0, b-5, c-3	10. a-0, b-5, c-3
5. a-5, b-0, c-3	11. a-3, b-0, c-5
6. a-3, b-0, c-5	12. a-0, b-3, c-5

IF YOU SCORED BETWEEN 45 AND 60 POINTS:

You're aces with anger.

In general, you're not an angry person. But when you do feel justifiable rancor you're quick to be aware of it and express your emotions appropriately. In other words, you've learned to react with "controlled anger"—the successful sibling of red-faced rage—which means that even when your adrenaline kicks in, you don't lash out. Instead, you use your instincts to produce the results you want, whether that means humbling a lout with witty repartee or cajoling a cantankerous airline agent into upgrading your ticket. More precisely, you've learned through experience that when anger isn't used to your advantage, it's toxic and destructive, so you aim your anger toward a specific goal rather than resorting to revenge. Since you understand and respect the potential of anger, you focus your powers on getting what you truly deserve. You deserve the best—and with your ability to handle hostility with finesse, you're likely to get it.

IF YOU SCORED BETWEEN 25 AND 44 POINTS:
You're hiding your hand.

If you've been raised in a family where anger isn't tolerated, where people don't fight fairly or are not allowed to express their anger, you're apt to believe that any expression of anger will spin you out of control. So you stifle it. But repressing hostility is like walking through a physical minefield. When you get angry, your body prepares for an "emergency" by kicking into the famed fight-or-flight response: blood pressure increases, heart rate rises, adrenaline surges, the senses sharpen. If anger is suppressed, there's no place for the body to release its stress. Instead, say health experts, life-threatening metabolic changes can occur, such as hardening of the arteries and weakening of the heart. You're also more at risk for bad habits, such as overeating, excessive drinking/smoking, as well as depression or anxiety attacks.

But blowing a gasket or pounding a pillow aren't the answers either. "Venting anger just keeps it alive," says Brad Bushman, PhD, a psychologist at Iowa State University. "People think it's going to work and when it doesn't, they become even more angry and frustrated." What to do?

- Confide in a friend.
- Engage your sense of humor.
- Go for a walk or try any form of exercise.
- Admit (out loud) that you're angry. It's the first and best step toward releasing the emotion and moving on.

IF YOU SCORED FEWER THAN 24 POINTS:
You're decked out.

You have no problem expressing your anger, which can be a good characteristic if you're in charge of the pique and can direct it to the light. But too often, your anger clouds your judgment; all that's left is the primitive urge to conquer and destroy. Which means: you're frequently pushed over the edge toward seeking revenge. The resulting damage to your relationships with colleagues, friends, and family can be substantial. What's more, after your anger is spent and you start to pick up the pieces, you're usually hit with the full force of guilt and remorse. Sound familiar? It's not a simple one-two step to rechoreograph what has been called "the dance of anger," but it's certainly worth the effort. Here are some techniques.

- Keep an "anger journal," recording your hostile feelings and actions. This will help identify your personal boiling points.

- Be brutal (on yourself). Question whether your anger is really justified and be ruthless in your self-evaluation.

- Seek a therapist. If self-help doesn't put your wrath under wraps, consider speaking with a behavior specialist who is trained in helping patients tame their tempests.

About 1 out of 7 Americans say they get angry just about every day. Surprisingly, men are 35 percent more likely than women to "seethe quietly."

4. Are you a perfectionist?

When it comes to doing things just right, do you always insist on perfection? "Knowing the answer can help you make the most of your time with the least amount of stress!" says Debbie Mandel, author of *Changing Habits*.

1. **Your signature is:**

   a. Full of ornate flourishes

   b. Always legible but not fancy

   c. Written quickly and casually

2. **At the last minute, you're asked to do something you've never done before— say, sing with the community chorus. You will probably:**

   a. Say no gracefully

   b. Say yes, but sing quietly

   c. Belt it out

3. **If your favorite antique teapot got a chip, you'd:**

   a. Turn it into a planter

   b. Repair it

   c. Keep using it as is

4. **How long does it usually take you to dress for work before leaving home?**

   a. Forty-five minutes or more

   b. Around half an hour

   c. Fewer than fifteen minutes

5. **You burn the bottom of a few home-baked cookies, so you:**

   a. Toss those and serve the rest

   b. Eat them yourself

   c. Stick the burned ones on the bottom and serve them all

6. **You apply lipstick with:**

   a. A liner and brush

   b. Directly from the tube

   c. You don't usually wear lipstick.

7. **Which would make you feel worse?**

   a. Walking into a fancy restaurant with a run in your stockings

   b. Getting stuck in traffic

   c. Missing a great sale!

Your Score

MOSTLY A'S:

You're the ultimate perfectionist.

Constantly striving to do everything just so, you prepare thoroughly, give it your all, and then take whatever you've accomplished to the next level. "For you, a job isn't finished until it's flawless," says Mandel. A born leader, you never settle for less than the best in yourself and know how to inspire the same high standards in everyone around you. But take note: too much perfectionism can paralyze you. When you get stuck, remind yourself, "Nobody is perfect" and give yourself permission to move on.

MOSTLY B'S:

You stand behind your name.

With your strong sense of integrity, when your name is attached to a project you care about, you'll devote yourself to making it perfect. For other, less important things, you can easily step back, delegating what you can and cutting yourself some slack if it doesn't come out just right. "If you make a mistake, you just learn from it and move on," says Mandel.

MOSTLY C'S:

You're a master compromiser.

Flexible and easygoing, you roll with the punches and can easily shift gears. That's because for you, it's about meeting deadlines and keeping everyone happy, not about being perfect all the time. A master juggler, you know how to find a balance between important and less-important projects, as well as between work and leisure.

5. How psychic are you?

"Everyone has some psychic powers," says Hans Christian King, author of *Stop Searching and Start Living*. Take this test to see how strong your ESP is.

1. **When the phone rings, you sense who's on the other end before you pick up:**

   a. Often

   b. Occasionally

   c. Only if you're expecting a call

2. **If you dreamed you discovered a new room in your home, you'd interpret this as a sign that:**

   a. Your mind is opening to new possibilities.

   b. Something unexpected is about to happen.

   c. You need more space.

3. **The lottery numbers you choose are usually:**

   a. Whatever pops into your head

   b. Lucky numbers

   c. Anniversaries or birthdays of loved ones

4. **When it comes to love at first sight, you:**

   a. Believe soul mates find each other this way

   b. Consider it possible

   c. Think lasting love takes time

5. **Have you ever had a premonition of something that subsequently took place?**

   a. Often

   b. Rarely

   c. Never

6. **When you were a young child, you spent most of your time:**

   a. Playing with an invisible friend

   b. Coloring or doing other creative activities

   c. Reading or watching television

7. **The last time you misplaced your keys, you relied on:**

   a. Your instincts or hunches to find them

   b. Memory to re-create an image of where you left them

   c. Someone to tell you where they were last seen

Your Score

MOSTLY A'S:

You're a true psychic.

"Natural psychics may realize in childhood their strong paranormal abilities," says King. You remember dreams vividly, know they hold insights about the future, and get a "feeling" about things before they happen. You may not always understand where these extrasensory signals are coming from, but you tend to trust them.

MOSTLY B'S:

You're a psychic detective.

Because you're tuned in to people and situations as well as your subconscious, you get signals others might overlook. You use your "sixth sense" to help you steer through life, picking up unspoken messages through subtle cues such as body language. "Keep on trusting your hunches and you'll sharpen your psychic powers!" says King.

MOSTLY C'S:

You're firmly grounded.

You make decisions based on what can be seen or proven—which is not to say you're closed to exploring new frontiers, only that your natural inclination is toward the ultra-rational. If you want to tap into your powers of ESP, "begin by trusting your inner feelings first before looking for the outside facts," says King.

Seventy-five percent of Americans believe they've had some kind of ESP experience.

6. What's your real age?

You invest wisely in your future, drive within the speed limit, and regularly view foreign films with scrawling subtitles. Are these the markers of true maturity, or merely superficial signs? Truth is, it's hard to tell. Most experts agree that real age is a tricky business; it's largely an attitude of mind. Thus, you can't calculate real age by the number of times you follow rules, make highbrow cultural choices, bite the bullet, or persevere through obstacles. Shakespeare wrote about the "seven ages of man," implying that we all move from cradle to grave in a series of uniform steps. But he might have generalized a bit too much. We do learn by experience, but some of us have to repeat a grade. Take this quiz to find out whether you're stuck in childhood, idling in adolescence, or gunning the gas as a savvy adult.

1. **When something goes wrong, your basic philosophy is:**

   a. What goes around comes around.

   b. I can learn from the experience.

   c. It's fate; I just have to ride the ups and downs.

2. **When you are confined to bed with a bad cold, you prefer to be:**

   a. Fussed over

   b. Left alone

   c. Brought some books and juice but basically left to your own devices

3. **When a randy teen movie like *Jackass* is released, you are likely to:**

   a. Hope it doesn't stay at your neighborhood theater for too long

   b. See it if nothing else is playing

   c. Be one of the first in line

4. **When angry, you are more likely to:**

   a. Express the reasons behind your feeling

   b. Breathe deeply and stifle your reaction

   c. Vent—it's the only way to let go

5. **Before making a major decision in your life, you:**

   a. Agonize over the alternative

   b. Make up your mind quickly and stick to it

   c. Think it over carefully, and then decide with as few regrets as possible

6. **If you were given a moderate sum of money (say, as much as you earn in a month) you would:**

   a. Save it

   b. Spend it on something you don't need but have wanted for a while

   c. Buy something practical

7. **You've arranged your dream holiday, but it's a month away. You:**

   a. Feel so excited that the waiting time until departure will be empty and drag on

   b. Spend a lot of time daydreaming about your upcoming trip

   c. Mark it on your calendar, but in the meantime get on with your life

8. **Do you tend to be rushed at the last minute because you've wasted time?**

   a. Sometimes.

   b. Rarely.

   c. Often.

9. **Have you ever stopped yourself from getting involved with someone because you feared rejection?**

   a. No.

   b. Occasionally.

   c. Often.

10. **A friend hurts your feelings. You:**

    a. Need at least a few hours before you can talk about it

    b. Want to tell her right away, on the spot

    c. May never say anything about it

11. **The person you most care about:**

    a. Needs you more than you do him or her

    b. Needs you about the same

    c. Doesn't need you as much as you do him or her

12. **Which of these qualities do you think is most important in a friend?**

    a. Shared values

    b. Reliability

    c. Good looks

13. **How did you choose your present job?**

    a. Your parents or teachers pushed it on you many years ago.

    b. It was all you could find.

    c. It's something you sought.

14. **When your boss tells the staff that people need to work harder, you're likely to assume that he or she:**

    a. Means everyone

    b. Is talking about your co-workers

    c. Is speaking directly to you

15. **How often do you take time off from work (other than scheduled vacations) just to have fun?**

    a. At least a few times a year

    b. Never!

    c. Maybe once in a while—but then I feel so guilty I can't enjoy myself.

Your Score

Give yourself the following number of points for each answer:

1. a-0, b-5, c-3	9. a-5, b-3, c-0
2. a-0, b-3, c-5	10. a-5, b-3, c-0
3. a-3, b-5, c-0	11. a-3, b-5, c-0
4. a-5, b-3, c-0	12. a-5, b-3, c-0
5. a-0, b-3, c-5	13. a-0, b-3, c-5
6. a-3, b-0, c-5	14. a-5, b-0, c-3
7. a-0, b-3, c-5	15. a-5, b-0, c-3
8. a-3, b-5, c-0	

IF YOU SCORED BETWEEN 65 AND 75 POINTS:
You are a postgraduate.

Whatever your age, you are an adult at heart. This means that your solutions to day-to-day problems and your general tactical approach to life are mature and realistic. You have a strong rational streak, hating pointless arguments and tending to reject idealism. You see yourself as essentially a powerful figure at least to the extent that you feel able to control yourself and care for others at the same time. If you are a parent, you are probably strongly aware of your responsibilities. Although you are steady, responsible, and as emotionally strong as the Rock of Gibraltar, there are drawbacks. If you ever question whether you're losing out on a bit of the fun and magic of life, the answer is probably yes. Take some regular time out just for you, whether it's to meditate or get a makeover. As little as one hour a week (though more is better) can make a major difference in your life. What more adult thing is there than letting go once in a while so you can recharge?

IF YOU SCORED BETWEEN 35 AND 64 POINTS:
You are a middle schooler.

With a score in this range, you are an adolescent at heart. It is characteristic of the adolescent personality that there is a conflict between a need—almost a crushing need—for independence and an equally overpowering need for support and protection. Just like you, the adolescent desires above all to break away from the confine of home and routine and yet, at the same time, has an underlying anxiety about the rigors of the world outside. Whatever your chronological age, this adolescent ambivalence is still a strong vein in your character. Though you tend to be realistic in assessing situations, your emotional range varies. You can turn from sunny to rottweiler mean in a minute. Possibly the strongest feature in your personality is your creative spirit. You hold the vision that all things are possible.

IF YOU SCORED FEWER THAN 34 POINTS:
You are back in kindergarten.

In all probability, you have a strong feeling of helplessness and a powerful need for emotional support—especially during critical times. What's more, you tend to be a pleaser; you crave approval. This may sound pretty negative, but not necessarily so. The childish aspect of your personality makes you unrealistic in lots of ways, but it could be that you feel happiness more keenly than more "mature" people do. You approach new situations with enthusiasm and zeal rather than fear. Although you're charming, you're also a bit irresponsible. This can be trying for those who expect you to be reliable, but not many people can stay mad at you for long. Gifted with a strong, spirited nature, you have the ability to bring out the best in others.

7. How flexible are you?

When life doesn't go as planned, do you get frazzled or go with the flow? "Studies show a link between flexibility and social or job success, not to mention lower stress levels and greater happiness," says Jennifer Reed Hawthorne, author of *The Soul of Success: A Woman's Guide to Authentic Power*. Take this quiz to see how flexible you really are.

1. **Have you ever gone to a different hairstylist when yours was unavailable?**

   a. Yes.

   b. No.

2. **You've planned a quiet day, but a friend asks you to baby-sit. You:**

   a. Agree. She wouldn't ask if she didn't really need you.

   b. Tell her you'd love to, but it's impossible.

3. **Have you ever broken an appointment without feeling guilty?**

   a. Yes.

   b. No.

4. **An hour before your dinner guests are due, you realize you're out of a crucial ingredient. You:**

   a. Use a substitute

   b. Put everything on hold and dash out to the supermarket

5. **They don't have the shoes you want in your size. You:**

   a. Choose a similar pair

   b. Ask the store to order them

6. **Your neighbor is nice, but tends to ramble. You:**

   a. Listen a bit, and then gracefully disengage

   b. Duck her as often as possible

7. **Have you ever let your husband do some decorating even though it wasn't exactly your taste?**

   a. Yes.

   b. No.

8. **Friends drop by without calling. You:**

   a. Are happy to see them

   b. Are not very happy because you prefer to have notice

Your Score

Give yourself 10 points for every "a" answer.

BETWEEN 70 AND 80 POINTS:
You're fabulously flexible.

For you, rolling with life's ups and downs is as natural as breathing. Confident and creative, you adapt to whatever comes along. "But repressing your true feelings when things go awry can lead to stress and health issues," warns Hawthorne. Instead…

- Listen to your body. Headaches, stomach discomfort, or insomnia may be your body's way of saying you're holding back on what you want or taking on too much to make things right. So shift gears or postpone something you don't want to do.

- Schedule fifteen minutes of "me" time. It's the first thing women like you give up. But a leisurely bath or manicure can go a long way toward reducing stress and reviving you for what's next!

BETWEEN 40 AND 60 POINTS:
You're a great compromiser.

Centered and serene, you equate flexibility with compromise. But you find it difficult to be flexible about things you cherish most. To keep the peace and still hold your ground:

- Translate what you hear by repeating it back with "I hear you saying…" Studies show this helps both parties stay open to all sides of an issue.

- Agree to disagree. It's okay to pick a few areas where you allow yourself to stand firm without feeling guilty!

30 POINTS OR LESS:
You crave consistency.

You know what you want—which is why routine is so important to you. "But by never going with the flow, you may be missing out on exciting possibilities," says Hawthorne. So:

- Say yes sometimes, even when you want to say no. It will lead you to consider new possibilities—the first step toward becoming more flexible.

- Try something new, whether it's a daring hairstyle or a different route to work. "Even small changes will help you become more flexible," says Hawthorne.

In a national survey, employers ranked the ability to compromise and be a team player as the number-one trait they look for in employees.

8. Discover the secrets you reveal in bed.

Even if you don't talk in your sleep, you're still saying something in bed—because your favorite sleeping position reveals secrets about how you see yourself and the world around you. "By observing thousands of subjects, we've discovered that an individual's preferred sleep position translates into a silent body language and offers concrete clues to personality," says Samuel Dunkell, MD, director of New York's Insomnia Medical Services and author of *Sleep Positions: Night Language of the Body*. Find your most frequent slumber position here and discover what helps you sleep at night.

ON YOUR BACK:
You have sky-high self-esteem.

A survey found that most Hollywood stars sleep on their backs—and no wonder! This position is typical of those who rate highest for self-esteem: the typical back sleeper is an outgoing optimist who shines in the limelight. Though you may not be famous, you're secure enough to chase your dreams with gusto. Even in your sleep, you face out toward the world.

IN THE FETAL POSITION:
You're a sensitive romantic.

Folks who favor the classic fetal position, with knees pulled up to the chest and chin tucked down, tend to be introspective, compassionate romantics. Whether you're rescuing a stray puppy or giving a friend a hug when she's down, your dreamy idealism makes the world a better place for you—and everyone else—to live.

ON YOUR STOMACH:
You've got a will of iron.

Most high-level managers sleep on their stomachs, and with good reason. Stomach-sleepers tend to be grounded, organized perfectionists who like to stay in control. That's why, whether you're sprawled on the bed or hugging a pillow to your chest, you sleep best when you're in full, face-to-face contact with the bed. With your will of iron and powerful strength of character, once you set your mind to something, it's as good as done.

ON YOUR SIDE:
You're adaptable.

If you're comfiest snoozing on your side, you're in the majority. It's a middle-of-the-road, see-every-side, flexible position favored by folks who are naturally able to adapt and compromise. No wonder you're the one to whom friends look for balanced advice. Open-minded and willing to listen, you gather all the information before making a decision—and this see-the-big-picture attitude means you adapt to any situation with ease.

YOU SWITCH POSITIONS ALL NIGHT:
You're an action-oriented go-getter.

Sleep doctors say we all switch positions at least twice during the night, but if you're on the move constantly, you've likely got energy to burn. A restless go-getter, you jump into projects with wholehearted enthusiasm, and although you sometimes burn out before the job is done, that's okay: your spark often ignites an even hotter flame elsewhere. You are eager to try new things such as exotic food or unusual perfume, and your boundless spirit keeps you moving forward.

31

The Top Three Sleeping Tips

· Roll up the shades and expose yourself to bright light as soon as you wake up. It will help regulate your natural biological clock.

· Read a boring book at night; thrillers and engaging novels will only keep you awake.

· Opt for toasty toes. Warm feet help you feel ready for rest. Either wear socks or try an old-fashioned hot water bottle.

9. How blissful are you?

Getting older means getting happier! Don't worry about wrinkles. A study of 540 people conducted by researchers at the University of Michigan found that the happiest folks are fifty years and over. The biggest reason? The wisdom and perspective they've gained through life experience.

1. Which of these statements most closely reflects your philosophy?

a. When one door closes, another opens.

b. You can't open the door without the golden key.

c. Some doors are better left locked.

2. After you awaken from a particularly vivid dream, you:

a. Record it in your journal, then shut the book and forget about it

b. Try to decipher its deeper meaning throughout the day

c. Consider it just a dream and let it pass

3. At last! A morning all to yourself! You:

a. Sleep late, breakfast in bed, then loll around the house in your bathrobe

b. Wake with the alarm, work out with your favorite exercise tape, eat a wholesome breakfast, and then catch up on some chores

c. Sleep for an extra thirty minutes, awaken rested and rejuvenated, stretch, dress, and then make a date to meet friends

4. What's your first reaction once you realize you've made a mistake?

a. You feel remorseful and repeatedly roll it around in your mind.

b. You try to learn from it.

c. You excuse yourself; you're only human.

5. **When you're a little short on funds, you:**

   a. Are aware of all you're missing and envious of those who have more

   b. Are still able to have a good time. After all, the best things in life are free.

   c. Are grateful for what you do have. So many people are much worse off than you are.

6. **You experience stress-related ailments, such as insomnia, stomach disorders, and headaches:**

   a. Never.

   b. Rarely.

   c. Frequently.

7. **On an average, how many hours do you sleep each night?**

   a. At least eight

   b. Between five and seven

   c. Fewer than five

8. **You think true happiness is:**

   a. Something we must work on to achieve

   b. Why we're alive

   c. An illusion

9. **In sexual matters, you more closely resemble a:**

   a. Tiger—willing, even anxious to take the lead

   b. Pussycat—docile and waiting to be stroked

   c. Chameleon—sensitive to a myriad of possibilities

10. **Your best friend is floating on Cloud Nine. She just met a great guy, got the job of her dreams, and, to top it all off, she won a raffle for a five-star spa vacation. Honestly, you are:**

    a. Horribly envious.

    b. Happy. She deserves it.

    c. Hungry. You renew your acquaintance with Ben & Jerry.

11. **Your relationship with your family is:**

    a. Close but not stifling

    b. Suffocating

    c. Estranged

12. **The man you are seeing hates to dance and it's one of the things you love most in life. You:**

    a. Turn up the stereo and dance to the music when at home alone

    b. Turn in your dancing shoes; you're willing to make sacrifices

    c. Turn to a friend and ask her to join you at the local hot spot

13. **Most of your friends are:**

    a. Givers. They are there for you when you need them.

    b. Takers. You're the one who is always offering to boost morale.

    c. A combination of both. You're there for one another depending on need.

14. **You're feeling amorous but your lover rejects your advances. You are:**

    a. Devastated and wondering what you did to turn him off

    b. Annoyed that your urge won't be satisfied, but you get over it

    c. Concerned that your partner might be feeling depressed or distracted

15. **How often do you put someone else's happiness before your own?**

    a. Whenever you can.

    b. Not as often as you should.

    c. Seldom.

Your Score

Give yourself the following number of points for each answer:

1. a-5, b-3, c-1	8. a-3, b-5, c-0
2. a-3, b-5, c-0	9. a-3, b-3, c-5
3. a-3, b-5, c-0	10. a-3, b-5, c-0
4. a-0, b-5, c-0	11. a-5, b-0, c-0
5. a-0, b-3, c-5	12. a-3, b-0, c-5
6. a-5, b-3, c-0	13. a-3, b-0, c-5
7. a-5, b-3, c-0	14. a-0, b-3, c-3
	15. a-5, b-3, c-0

IF YOU SCORED BETWEEN 60 AND 75 POINTS:
You're boundlessly blissful.

The Dalai Lama says, "The very motion of life is toward happiness," and truly, that's the road you're traveling. You like your life, have the ability to enjoy it, and possess a basic sense of well-being. This means you have a willingness to accept what can't be changed, to learn from your mistakes, and to alter those circumstances you can control. Without fear, you open your heart to others and eagerly seek life's many opportunities. And surprisingly, you're not alone in your ability to experience inner joy. Despite the media's barrage of bad news and the increase in use of prescribed antidepressants, according to David Meyers, PhD, a professor of psychology at New Hope University in Holland, Michigan, 80 percent of us are innately joyous. In fact, we're genetically programmed to feel good. Happiness, researchers also tell us, is contagious, so it's not surprising that friends and family seek to stand within your golden light.

IF YOU SCORED BETWEEN 30 AND 59 POINTS:
You're basically content.

The dark clouds have descended on you more than you'd like, but you always feel that deep inside there's a silver lining. More important, you know that happiness is something to work toward. Even when you feel short changed in your relationships or career, you gravitate toward those activities that help you change the course of your mood. Optimism, researchers tell us, is a "learned skill." Whereas pessimists may complain, optimists focus on solving their problems. When you feel yourself sliding into negativity, you consciously try to change your course to a more positive one. You've experienced both the highs and lows of life, and that has given you the ability to empathize with others. This trait is invaluable in creating deep and lasting relationships.

IF YOU SCORED FEWER THAN 29 POINTS:
You could use a boost.

You've had many disappointments in your life and feel deeply dissatisfied, especially in the arena of relationships. As a result, a sort of hopelessness has settled into your psyche. But scientists and spiritual leaders point to specific ways you can elevate your level of happiness. First of all, there's a physical connection to our emotional life. Researchers confirm that too little sleep can lead to depression, so aim for a good eight hours each night. When you awake in the morning, simply smile—as suggested by the popular Vietnamese Buddhist teacher Thich Nhat Hanh. Psychologist MaryAnn Troiani, PhD, coauthor, with psychologist Michael Mercer, of *Spontaneous Optimism: Proven Strategies for Health, Prosperity & Happiness*, suggests standing straight, since good posture improves bad moods. Exercise three times weekly and fill your life with simple pleasures. Don't wait to get joy from big projects like vacations or major purchases. That kind of happiness is temporary and can leave you feeling deflated. Tell yourself you deserve to be happy (You do!), and then give yourself a chance to feel the bliss.

10. Do you have a green thumb?

Studies show that some of us are more likely than others to grow a lovely garden or keep our indoor plants thriving. "Patience, intuition, flexibility, attention to detail, and optimism" are essential, says landscape architect Julie Moir Messervy, author of *The Inward Garden*.

1. **Do you ever have a sixth sense about things?**

   a. Often

   b. Occasionally

   c. Never

2. **If someone is speaking very slowly during a conversation, you're likely to:**

   a. Listen carefully until the person finishes his or her thought

   b. Try your best to pay attention

   c. Jump in and politely move the speaker along

3. **You would describe your handwriting as:**

   a. Elegant—you take time to make it beautiful.

   b. Precise—with every *t* crossed and every *i* dotted.

   c. A hurried scrawl

4. **Of these, your favorite flower is:**

   a. Orchid

   b. Lily

   c. Rose

5. **When a friend calls to cancel dinner plans, you:**

   a. Understand that things come up

   b. Feel disappointed but figure there's a good reason for the cancellation

   c. Feel a bit annoyed about the empty spot in your day

6. **When faced with a new situation, you're usually:**

   a. Curious

   b. Courageous

   c. Cautious

7. Are you a good multitasker?

  a. No. I prefer to put all my energy into one thing at a time.

  b. Sort of. I can juggle two or three things okay, but anything more is too much.

  c. Yes. The busier I am, the more I get done.

8. You prefer to:

  a. Bake a cake from scratch

  b. Make it from a mix

  c. Buy it in a shop

Your Score

MOSTLY A'S:

You've got a natural green thumb!

With traits like patience, attention to detail, and flexibility, you have what it takes to cultivate a thriving garden or a house full of healthy plants. "Green-thumbers have a special desire to nurture, along with the ability to devote the time and concentration to care for growing plants. Plus, they have an intuitive knack for knowing just what flowers will thrive and where they should be planted," says Messervy. And you can expand your flower power even more by:

- Planting a specialty garden, such as perennial, rock, or herb, or add more exotic and challenging plants to your existing garden. It's a sure way to build your gardening know-how.

- Treating yourself to some quality gardening gear such as the latest weeders, mulchers, or a comfy seat to save your knees and make you feel like the queen of green.

MOSTLY B'S:

You've got green potential.

No question about it, you love plants and have the optimism it takes to make them grow, but still, your results are hit or miss. One reason: Your drive to get it right keeps you from trusting your instincts. Plus, your cautious nature makes you a little afraid to take risks. "But desire and interest are all it takes," says Messervy. Here are other ways to boost your growing confidence:

- Let the experts get you started. Begin with the prepotted plants that simply require full sunlight and daily watering and then add your own touches as the garden takes off.

- Don't be hard on yourself if the results don't live up to your expectations. Even for the best gardeners, it can be trial-and-error.

MOSTLY C'S:

Stick to silk flowers!

You're a real go-getter with a busy schedule, and with your jam-packed day, there's little time left for plants. But there are real benefits to having them around, especially for high-energy women like you. "Plants can reduce stress; even lower blood pressure," says Messervy. Here are easy ways to add some green to your life.

- Buy plants that require little care, such as cactus or bamboo.

- Head outside for lunch. Just looking at greenery can provide many of the same stress-relieving benefits.

11. What's in your family room?

"Everything about the space you create for yourself reflects your real identity," says Winifred Gallagher, author of *House Thinking*. Take this quiz and find out what your family room reveals.

1. **Your walls are:**
   a. Painted in white or pastel colors
   b. Painted in deep hues, such as red, blue, or green
   c. Wallpapered or paneled

2. **Your coffee table is made primarily of:**
   a. Glass, metal, or plastic
   b. Marble
   c. Wood

3. **Your floor covering is:**
   a. Bare wood
   b. Wall-to-wall carpeting
   c. A large area rug

4. **The one extra that would make your family room perfect is:**
   a. State-of-the-art entertainment center
   b. Fun bar area where you could offer refreshments
   c. Cozy window seat

5. **Which of these would you most prominently display on your coffee table?**
   a. Big picture book
   b. Candles or a candy dish
   c. Flowers or a plant

6. **Your window treatments are:**
   a. Simple panels
   b. Draperies with a valance
   c. Blinds or shades

7. **Your main lighting source is:**
   a. Floor lamps
   b. Table lamps
   c. Ceiling fixtures

Your Score

MOSTLY A'S:

Your family room says, "You reach for the stars."

"Modern and elegant, your family room reveals your desire to be the best at whatever you do," says Gallagher. Clean and clutter-free, your space helps you stay focused on your goals. Never one to settle for less than you desire, you map out a plan and move full-speed ahead until you achieve it.

Your family room says, "You're the life of the party."

"You go out of your way to create a warm space, which is probably why friends and family prefer your house for get-togethers," says Gallagher. Naturally outgoing and witty, you're a born hostess who knows how to put everyone at ease and add the special touches that make for a fun time.

Your family room says, "You're a deep thinker."

From the books you keep close by to the quiet corner you create for yourself, your family room shows that you're a compassionate soul—and a true thinker. "Genuinely spiritual, you consider your family room a sanctuary, a place to retreat from daily stresses and think about what matters most," says Gallagher.

12. Do you need more quiet time?

1. **If you could add one more room to your home, it would be:**

   a. A room to call your own

   b. A rec room

2. **When your eyes pop open in the morning, your first thoughts involve:**

   a. The day's most urgent chore

   b. The details of your last dream

3. **You have a hard time saying no without feeling guilty:**

   a. True

   b. False

4. **You're more likely to fantasize about being:**

   a. Transported to a romantic hideaway

   b. Whisked off to a gala event

5. **The last time you stayed late to play catch-up at work was:**

   a. Last night

   b. A few months ago

6. **You feel lonely:**

   a. Rarely

   b. Often

7. **You prefer stories that are packed with:**

   a. Intrigue and romance

   b. Drama and thrills

8. **When finishing up a job, you're eager to:**

   a. Tie up all the loose ends

   b. Move on to something new

9. **Talking to strangers:**

   a. Exhausts you

   b. Energizes you

10. **At the zoo, you'd be more likely to visit the area housing:**

   a. The contemplative giraffe

   b. The boisterous chimpanzees

11. **If a discussion becomes heated, you're more likely to:**

   a. Try and end it diplomatically

   b. Stick to your guns

12. **You try to shop during off hours and on weekdays to avoid the crush.**

   a. Agree

   b. Disagree

Nearly half of wives say their husbands get more time to themselves than they do.

Your Score

Note: If your score falls somewhat evenly between the two categories, read both descriptions, since you share characteristics of both types.

MOSTLY A'S:
Shhhhh!

Short on time, long on work, everyone you know seems to need a piece of you—no wonder you often feel so drained and exhausted by the end of the day! Maybe it's time to stop putting other people's demands first; allowing even fifteen minutes a day to soak in a warm bath or scribble down your thoughts will help you recharge your battery. You'll be amazed at how much better you feel—and how much more you'll be capable of!

MOSTLY B'S:
Turn up the volume, please!

Your hectic schedule might leave others longing for some solitude, but you're such a social sort that it has you feeling deprived of what you need most: the stimulation of other people's company! Try delegating part of your responsibilities to others, taking on group rather than solo projects, or diving into a hobby that requires two pairs of hands—and you'll be smiling more than ever.

13. Lessening stress— it's an art!

Want to unwind? The pictures you hang on your walls could help! We're instinctively drawn to visual images that make us feel relaxed and happy. "Art triggers a strong emotional reaction," explains New York City art expert and graphic designer Laurel Marx. "That's why you'll only choose images for your walls that resonate positively within you." Pick the kind of painting you would enjoy most and see what enhances your inner calm.

AN ABSTRACT:
You're a creative dynamo!

"People who are drawn to abstracts are crafts-people who find calm in unraveling why things are the way they are," explains Marx. Psychologists say that those with artistic temperaments are naturally analytical, "which is why you enjoy figuring out how things work, whether it's someone else's art or your own creative projects!" And there's an added bonus: activities such as knitting or painting provide a distraction from daily stresses, so the day-to-day hassles just drift away!

A BLACK-AND-WHITE PHOTOGRAPH:
You're a sensual sophisticate!

Having one of those days? Chances are you're dreaming about a bubble bath or a facial. "Folks who appreciate black-and-white photographs tend to be the most tuned into physical realities like touch and smell," says Marx. You know there's no hiding from those little aches and pains that go along with stress—and you do something about it! Good for you! According to research, pampering treatments ease anxiety and reduce stress hormones. So, fill the tub and get ready to wash away the cares of the day.

A MOVIE POSTER:
You're an outgoing social butterfly!

"Movie poster lovers release tension by socializing and having fun!" says Marx. The reason: Movie lovers relate to the characters on screen and enjoy bringing a similar energy to their own lives. The good news is that being a social butterfly can add years to your life. Studies show that strong friendships help keep people healthier and happier.

A FAMOUS MASTERPIECE:
You're an introspective intellectual!

"People who favor masterpieces are able to shed the stresses of the day by looking at a familiar work of art, reading a book, or listening to music," says Marx. When the world gets to be too much, you shut it out by turning inward—and that's where you find harmony.

A LANDSCAPE:

You're a savvy realist!

"People who are drawn to outdoor scenes have an innate ability to balance their lives," says Marx. The reason: "These images serve as a reminder that no matter how stressed you are, there's more to life than the problems of the moment." Why? Because they restore your perspective by showing you the world outside your personal problems—and that grounds you.

Impressionist painter Vincent van Gogh was poor—but his Portrait of Dr. Gachet is one of the most expensive paintings ever auctioned, at $85.2 million!

14. How strong is your willpower?

When temptation mounts, can you resist—or do you give in easily? "Willpower is about tapping into your inner strength and channeling it," says psychologist Martha Pieper, PhD, author of *Addicted to Unhappiness: Free Yourself from the Moods and Behaviors that Undermine Relationships, Work and the Life You Want.* Take this quiz to discover the key to your personal resolve.

1. **You found your dream dress at the mall, but the price is way out of your budget. You:**

   a. Charge it or put it on layaway

   b. Look for something you can afford

2. **You overhear a juicy bit of gossip at work. You:**

   a. Share it with your closest colleague, swearing her to secrecy

   b. Keep it to yourself

3. **You stick to your to-do list:**

   a. Rarely

   b. Most of the time

4. **You buy a candy bar, but can you eat just half and save the rest for later?**

   a. No

   b. Sure

5. **Do you ever look at the final page of a book before finishing it?**

   a. Sometimes

   b. Never

6. **You notice that your teenage daughter has left her journal out. You:**

   a. Speed-read it from cover to cover

   b. Resist peeking

7. **How often do you grab an item at the last minute, while in line at the super-market check-out?**

   a. Frequently

   b. Rarely

8. **Your credit cards are:**

   a. Maxed to the limit

   b. Paid in full monthly, or with a very low balance

9. **You start watching a favorite movie but realize it ends late and you have to wake up early. You:**

   a. Stay up until the very end

   b. Shut it off and go to sleep

Your Score

Give yourself 10 points for every "a" answer and 5 points for every "b."

BETWEEN 75 AND 90 POINTS:
Whatever you set your mind to, you accomplish, never letting temptation steer you off course. "But sometimes such ironclad resolve means you might be missing out on life's enjoyable moments," says Pieper. To loosen up without losing your self-discipline:

- Give your inner perfectionist the day off by focusing on the words, "Nobody's perfect!" Repeating this affirmation gives you permission to cut yourself some slack.

- Say yes at least once in a while. By rewarding yourself now and then, you'll be twice as excited about the next task at hand.

BETWEEN 50 AND 74 POINTS:
"Your ability to adapt to situations when they arise keeps stress to a minimum and helps you accept the fact that you can't control everything in your life," points out Pieper. You're also clear about setting priorities—which for you means putting comfort and happiness first. It's why your willpower is weakest when it comes to forfeiting fun. Here's how you can set limits while still enjoying yourself:

- Keep it light. Since your priority is enjoyment, turn even routine tasks into pleasant activities by playing music in the background or taking a renewing break by walking.

- Grab a supportive buddy. A colleague who shares your goals boosts both your morale and resolve!

49 POINTS OR LESS:
Your live-in-the-moment attitude means you have a tough time saying no when something intriguing or tempting comes along. But it's never too late to learn to flex your willpower muscles. To get started:

- Take it "one day at a time." That way, if you slip up, you can forgive yourself and begin anew without feeling defeated.

- Set reachable goals. You'll be more likely to be successful.

What's the hardest food to resist on a diet? Chocolate was voted number one, ahead of cheese and chips.

15. What's your ideal hobby?

"Hobbies make us happier, healthier, and stress-free—and research proves it!" says Laurie Beth Jones, author of *The Four Elements of Success*. This test tells you where your true talents lie.

1. **When you go on vacation, you usually buy:**
   a. Lots of fun souvenirs
   b. Maybe a T-shirt
   c. Postcards only

2. **The shoes you wear most often are:**
   a. Cute pumps
   b. Sneakers
   c. Loafers or slip-ons

3. **The wardrobe item you can't get enough of is:**
   a. Handbags
   b. Shoes
   c. Sweaters

4. **On average, your morning make-up routine takes:**
   a. Over five minutes
   b. Five minutes or less
   c. No time. You don't usually wear makeup.

5. **On a weekend with family you'd rather play:**
   a. Charades
   b. Miniature golf
   c. Monopoly

6. **The rooms in your home are painted:**
   a. A variety of different colors
   b. Mostly white
   c. Soft neutrals

7. **The TV anchor you most admire is:**
   a. Katie Couric
   b. Campbell Brown
   c. Diane Sawyer

Your Score

MOSTLY A'S:

You're the crafty type.

Wildly creative, your perfect hobby would tap into your inner artist. You'd enjoy whipping up a culinary masterpiece, redecorating a room, or compiling a scrapbook. Because you're easily bored, you like to dabble in lots of activities, moving on after you've mastered something. "Artistic types find inspiration and renewed self-confidence in experimenting—and that boost gives you energy to face real-life challenges, too," says Jones.

MOSTLY B'S:
You're a mover and a shaker.

An on-the-go type, you'd benefit most from a hobby that lets you work off some of that boundless energy. Think gardening, dancing, hiking, yoga, or tai chi—activities that shift your focus. "Anything that lets you dig right in, concentrate, and keep moving will encourage you to stay inspired and ultimately more relaxed," says Jones.

MOSTLY C'S:
You're a quiz whiz.

Since you have a mind that's always buzzing, there's no better hobby for you than brain games—such as trivia contests, crossword puzzles, sudoku, computer games, chess, or even reading a good whodunit. "People with active minds find real release in brain teasers," says Jones.

Looking for a hobby? Log on to www.findmeahobby.com and explore hundreds!

16. What does your favorite sleepwear reveal about you?

Surprise! What you wear to bed each night reveals a lot more than it covers up! "At bedtime we naturally choose what feels right and comfortable on the deepest, most subconscious level," says Linda Rae Tepper, co-owner of Nick and Nora, a world-renowned sleepwear design studio. So pick your favorite dreamtime duds—and wake up to the real you!

TRADITIONAL NIGHTGOWN:
You're a modern romantic.

Traditional women's nightgowns, including romantic floor-length ensembles, baby dolls, and shorties, "have a reputation for sexiness, but most of them are relaxed and allow for lots of movement," explains Tepper. If you're drawn to them, you enjoy being feminine and pretty—but you're also practical and modern. This practicality reveals itself in most areas of your life, from how you raise your kids to the way you handle your career. It's this unique blend of whimsy and common sense that friends and family find so endearing.

CAMISOLE, CHEMISE, OR TEDDY:
You're a real charmer.

"Comfortable in your own skin, you're at ease enough within yourself to know that beauty is an attitude—not a size or shape," says Tepper.

Your charismatic personality allows you to charm everyone: sales clerks, co-workers, even your kids' teachers. Since you know that the secret of popularity is confidence, you never lack for friends, and your happy demeanor is contagious: you make others feel just as good. Pals know that no gathering is complete unless you're invited, so your social calendar (and your heart) is always full.

FLANNEL PAJAMAS:
You're an open book.

Here's betting you'd make a terrible poker player! Why? "Flannel pajama-wearers are so at ease and feel so relaxed, it's almost impossible for them to be anything but upfront and honest," says Tepper. This means that no matter what mood you're in, your emotions show! Never one for subterfuge or deceit, you're so sincere that even people who don't know you feel comfortable and cozy in your presence, and they're quick to put their trust in you. But the fact that you're open doesn't mean you're naive. You have an uncanny ability to spot insincerity in others—and you have no problem telling those who are trying to deceive you just what you think of them!

YOUR BIRTHDAY SUIT:
You're a spirited idealist.

"Women who go to bed in the buff are idealistic, creative thinkers," says Tepper. Your willingness to do away with sleepwear shows you're a natural leader ready to make a change. Whether it's pushing for a new school reading program or starting a charity drive, your ideas are often the beginning of something original and wonderful. And your innovative attitude doesn't change when you're at play. Friends know you're just as likely to throw a surprise party as you are to drop by for coffee—and it's this spontaneity that they admire so much.

OVERSIZE T-SHIRT:
You've got your eye on the prize.

"A big T-shirt is a no-fuss way to sleep: it's comfy; it's easy to care for, and, if you add a pair of sweats, it's versatile enough to wear to the gym," says Tepper. Why the emphasis on ease and simplicity? Because you're striving for important goals, whether it's rising up the workplace ladder or saving for your kid's college fund—or even going back to college yourself. Focused and determined, you go after what you want with gusto. But don't forget to take time to relax. Slip into the comfy T-shirt, stretch out on the couch, and escape into your favorite magazine. You deserve it.

17. How does procrastinating help you?

Procrastination isn't just about putting off work! Take this quiz, developed with consultant Kerul Kassel, founder of www.stopprocrastinatingnow.com, and uncover the hidden strengths behind your procrastination style!

1. **You deal with paper clutter by:**

   a. Stacking it in piles; you know where everything is.

   b. Waiting until it accumulates and then creating a new filing system

   c. Filing things away every day

2. **You're planning to tackle a big project when something fun comes up. You:**

   a. Reschedule your project and have fun

   b. Get at least half done, then leave

   c. Finish the project completely before you go

3. **When it comes to paying taxes, you usually:**

   a. Mail them right on the due date

   b. Need an extension

   c. File your return early

4. **Unexpected guests call to say they're on their way. You:**

   a. Do some frantic tidying up

   b. Suggest meeting somewhere else, like a coffee shop

   c. Feel the house is presentable enough

5. **Your exercise program is basically:**

   a. Running from chore to chore

   b. Constantly changing. You haven't found one you love yet.

   c. Going well

6. **Your most productive time of day is:**

   a. Late afternoon or evening

   b. Varied

   c. Morning or early afternoon

7. **Today's to-do list has:**

   a. Not been checked yet; you're too busy!

   b. You feeling overwhelmed

   c. Items crossed off as you go

Your Score

MOSTLY A'S:

You're a juggler.

Full of energy and drive, you try to accomplish so much every day that you often need to put a few things off for later. "But you enjoy the thrill of accomplishing more than even you think you can," says Kassel. Her advice: Minimize stress by not putting more than six items on your daily to-do list.

MOSTLY B'S:
You're a perfectionist.

You wonder: If you can't do it with excellence, why bother? And it's that impulse that sometimes has you putting things off. "You love to tackle things when you can give them your full attention," says Kassel. She suggests that to keep the pressure from building when your inner critic chirps in, just remind yourself that nobody's perfect.

MOSTLY C'S:
You're methodical.

When you've got a list of things to do, you give each your full attention, not moving on until you're finished. To outsiders, it may seem as though you're putting off other things on the list, "but odds are, you set priorities, then pace yourself so you don't burn out," says Kassel. What you end up with are solid results with very little stress.

18. What's your "smart scent?"

Find the aroma that perfectly matches your personality, and you can unlock the secret to a sharper mind, says aromatherapist Juliana Lipe of Essencia Aromatics.

1. **If you decided to try a low-carb diet, you'd probably:**

   a. Read a book about it

   b. Just cut out bread and pasta and see what happens

   c. Join a program or ask for advice from a friend who's tried it

2. **The last book you read was a:**

   a. Self-help or how-to book

   b. Memoir

   c. Novel

3. **The hobby that most appeals to you is:**

   a. Photography

   b. Painting

   c. Scrapbooking or quilting

4. **Which of these reality shows would you be most likely to watch?**

   a. *Survivor*

   b. *American Idol*

   c. *The Bachelor*

5. **If stuck in traffic you'd be most likely to:**

   a. Strategize another way to get where you're going

   b. Look for a better lane and hope the traffic cleared up soon

   c. Put on your favorite CD and relax

6. **When it comes to vacations, you usually:**

   a. Plan well in advance and do lots of research

   b. Wait until the last minute, knowing it will all work out

   c. Return to your favorite place once a year

7. You feel most energized in the:

a. Morning

b. Afternoon

c. Evening

Your Score

MOSTLY A'S:

Your concentration booster is FLORALS.

Forward-thinking multitaskers like you benefit most from floral scents such as geranium, jasmine, lavender, and rose—either in fresh flowers, candles, or essential oils. "Florals offer a balancing effect for go-getter types," says Lipe. "They not only soothe and calm, but also enhance inner strength so you can zero in on your priorities."

MOSTLY B'S:

Your concentration booster is FRESH HERBS.

You're an idealist who believes that where there's a will, there's a way. Having earthy, herbal aromas on hand will keep you grounded so you can concentrate on finding practical solutions to whatever comes along. "Scents such as basil, fennel, rosemary, and thyme enhance mental clarity while keeping your upbeat spirit focused," Lipe explains.

MOSTLY C'S:

Your concentration booster is CITRUS.

Sensitive and ultra-feminine, romantic types like you follow their hearts when it comes to making decisions. To sharpen your mind, keep lots of citrus scents handy. "Fresh fragrances like lemon, lime, orange, and grapefruit boost your energy and heighten your awareness so you'll always stay one step ahead of the game," say Lipe.

19. Are you a risk taker?

Like living on the edge? Or are you more at ease with the safe and secure? "Your comfort level with taking risks offers insight into your personality—as well as your prospects for success," says Bill Treasurer, author of *Right Risk*. This test will help you determine your risk-taking level.

1. I've changed jobs more than once in the last five years:

a. True

b. False

2. I buy lottery or raffle tickets:

a. Frequently

b. Rarely or never

3. I usually wake up by:

a. My inner clock

b. My alarm clock

4. Would you ride in a hot-air balloon if you had the opportunity?

a. Absolutely!

b. No way!

5. **The last time I bought an article of clothing it was:**

   a. In a store, after trying it on in the dressing room

   b. Through a catalog or Web site after studying the picture

6. **I drive more than seven miles over the speed limit on highways.**

   a. Frequently

   b. Rarely

7. **I'm more apt to look over a restaurant's menu and order:**

   a. Something that sounds unusual and different

   b. A favorite I know I'll enjoy

8. **I change my look:**

   a. Frequently

   b. Rarely

9. **The last time I had to make a major decision in my life, I:**

   a. Made up my mind quickly and stuck to it

   b. Agonized over the alternatives

10. **When it comes to sharing details about my life, I'm:**

    a. An open book

    b. A bit hard to read

Your Score

IF YOU ANSWERED "A" TO 7 OR MORE QUESTIONS:

You're a high roller.

Your fearlessness keeps things exciting and has led to some terrific twists of fate. To ensure a happy ending for all your risks, experts advise a quick time-out before jumping in. And to make sure you don't step on any toes, talk over your decisions with those who will be affected by them. This will help you learn from your mistakes—a crucial skill for a brilliant risk taker.

IF YOU ANSWERED "A" TO 4 TO 6 QUESTIONS:

You look before you leap.

Before you make a decision, you weigh the pros and cons carefully. That's typically a smart move, but sometimes thinking for too long means you miss the boat. Remember the adage "She who hesitates is lost." Trust your instincts! Research shows that for conscientious types like you, your hunches are right 90 percent of the time.

IF YOU ANSWERED "A" TO FEWER THAN 3 QUESTIONS:

You're supercautious.

Psychologists call you "risk averse," meaning you're most comfortable when you can see the road ahead of you. To learn to let go a little more, the next time something risky presents itself ask yourself, what's the worst thing that could happen if it doesn't work out? "To be a risk-taker, you have to accept messiness," says Treasurer.

20. Do you have healthy self-esteem?

Around the age of two, we begin to devote energy—much of it unconscious—to building an image of ourselves that we find personally acceptable and acceptable to the outside world. Our satisfaction with this personal image is defined as "self-esteem." Those with high self-esteem are confident. They not only admire their own physical characteristics—hair, facial features, weight, and height—but also believe that they possess the power to control their own destinies. Usually flexible and compassionate, these confident souls are willing to accept responsibility, forgiving themselves as well as others when necessary. Conversely, those with low self-esteem give off a sense of powerlessness. Despite the attainment of beauty, money, or success, they feel like frauds. Though continually seeking reassurance from the outside world, they never get enough. Worse, when things go awry, it's always someone else's fault: uncaring parents, conniving colleagues, or a bad hairdresser. Most of us fall somewhere in between the high and low end on the self-esteem scale: there are certain areas in which we feel confident, others where we wish we had a boost.

In the words of the great philosopher and writer Goethe, "It's a great mistake to fancy oneself greater than one is—and worse still to value oneself at less than one is worth." This quiz will help you identify your level of self-esteem and offer some strategies for balancing it.

1. **The way you walk is best described as:**

   a. Straight backed, with bouncy movements. Companions frequently ask you to slow down.

   b. A bit slumped and "dreamy." You walk at a leisurely pace, often finding objects on the ground.

   c. Occasionally lax, but mostly disciplined. You move with grace and ease.

2. **You're sipping coffee at the local café when your favorite movie star sidles up. You:**

   a. Feel butterflies in your stomach but make an effort to appear blasé

   b. Duck behind your newspaper—and regret it for the rest of your life

   c. Flash your thousand-watt smile

3. **Your wardrobe is:**

   a. Stupendous! You're a shopping junkie and your closets are crammed with the latest looks.

   b. Spare. You're all about the simple basics.

   c. Selective. Your diverse personal style takes you instantly from funky to high fashion.

4. **You're feeling emotionally and physically blah when an acquaintance says, "You've never looked better!" What's your reaction? You:**

   a. Wonder what she wants

   b. Assume she's being nice

   c. Appreciate the compliment—you can use it

5. **You're at a public meeting or lecture and you want to ask a question. You:**

   a. Take the first possible opportunity to stand up and fire away

   b. Rehearse the words in your head until you feel confident enough to raise your hand

   c. Probably don't dare ask

6. **When venturing into the unknown, you agree most with which writer?**

   a. Erica Jong, who said, "The trouble is, if you don't risk anything, you risk even more."

   b. Charlotte Brontë, who said, "Look twice before you leap."

   c. Colette, who said, "You will do foolish things, but do them with enthusiasm."

7. **Do others perceive you as strong even though you might be feeling insecure?**

   a. Often, yes

   b. Sometimes, but not always

   c. Rarely

8. **Some people consider themselves lucky; others think life dealt them a crummy hand. You:**

   a. Believe you can overcome any lack of luck with bountiful energy and clever strategies

   b. Feel like you were born lucky. You've aced it.

   c. Wish you could reshuffle the deck and get some decent cards

9. **You walk into a party of strangers and everyone is situated in groups, deep in conversation. You:**

   a. Walk around until you feel comfortable, then zero in on a cluster and introduce yourself

   b. Grab a drink, prop yourself against the wall, and make eye contact with anyone who looks in your direction

   c. Decide to leave

10. **Do you call your parents by their first names?**

    a. Yes. You're an adult.

    b. Yes—but only because they suggested it.

    c. No. It sounds disrespectful.

11. **When someone appears to dislike you, you:**

    a. Wonder if you did something to offend her

    b. Think she must be jealous of you

    c. Accept philosophically that you can't win them all

12. **When making love, you prefer to keep the lights:**

    a. Dimmed

    b. Out

    c. On

13. **If your date wore a velvet vest that made him look like Peter Rabbit, you'd:**

    a. Give him a hint by handing him a carrot

    b. Hide in a cabbage patch so you don't have to be seen with him

    c. Walk arm-in-arm without so much as a nibble of embarrassment

14. **An acquaintance quarrels with you over what you consider to be unreasonable grounds. You:**

    a. Try to meet her halfway

    b. Straight out tell her how you see things

    c. Feel hurt and angry but do everything you can to avoid a confrontation

15. **A colleague asks you for a favor that requires a fair amount of time—something you don't have. You:**

    a. Feel annoyed but grudgingly help her out

    b. Explain that your time is too tight and offer your apology

    c. Decide to do it. If you don't, it could create resentment.

Your Score

Give yourself the following number of points for each answer:

1. a-5, b-0, c-3	9. a-5, b-3, c-0
2. a-3, b-0, c-5	10. a-5, b-3, c-0
3. a-0, b-3, c-5	11. a-3, b-0, c-5
4. a-0, b-3, c-5	12. a-3, b-0, c-5
5. a-5, b-3, c-0	13. a-3, b-0, c-5
6. a-5, b-0, c-3	14. a-3, b-5, c-0
7. a-0, b-3, c-5	15. a-0, b-3, c-5
8. a-5, b-3, c-0	

IF YOU SCORED BETWEEN 50 AND 75 POINTS:
You have SOARING self-esteem.

Some people are born with a powerful sense of self-esteem; they have a natural ability to rebound from obstacles, even difficult childhoods. But with a score this high, you more than likely grew up in a supportive environment with adults and siblings who freely praised you. As a result, you know your own feelings and handle them well. Whenever you're down, you're able to come up with a solution to make yourself feel better. The reason: you rarely rely on others to create your reality. Thanks to this high level of self-esteem, you're not only comfortable enough with yourself to be playful and open to new experiences, you don't put blame on anyone—including yourself. You're willing to look at your mistakes, take responsibility and feel grateful for the opportunity to learn and grow from them. However, if you feel as if you always excel at your relationships and your job, take a good, hard look at yourself. You might be overestimating your prowess. No one is that perfect. The only way to truly feel good about yourself is to embrace the real you—flaws and all.

IF YOU SCORED BETWEEN 25 AND 49 POINTS:
You have SLIPPERY self-esteem.

Most of the time, your feelings and self-confidence serve you well. You're able to identify problems, deal with them, and move on—though not in all aspects of your life. Those times when your self-esteem falls short could be the result of old behavior patterns. Certain situations can trigger childhood scenarios, and if you haven't worked them through yet, your self-esteem will suffer. If, for example, your father always criticized you, it may be difficult for you to accept any kind of feedback from your partner—either positive or negative—without feeling defensive or resentful. You can change this cycle by becoming conscious of your reactions. Instead of letting anger take over, direct your energy positively. When a problem arises, think, "Okay, I have the power to resolve it." Also, try not to be so self-critical. Of course you feel a temporary twinge of jealousy or envy when a friend or colleague excels. Who wouldn't? Just don't judge yourself. Make your mantra "Nobody is perfect. Everybody is perfect." The next time you open your heart to forgiveness, be the first on the receiving line.

IF YOU SCORED FEWER THAN 24 POINTS:
You have SAGGING self-esteem.

While to the outside world you may appear confident, it should come as no surprise to you that inwardly you lack self-esteem. You compare yourself unfavorably to friends and colleagues by setting up an imaginary competition that you're bound to lose. This self-imposed pressure inevitably leaves you feeling dissatisfied with yourself. Since you're hardly ever happy with your personal performance, you drive yourself relentlessly, motivated by a need to accomplish everything in order not to be a complete failure. Also, you tend to make statements like "I'm worthless" or "I'll never be a success," which eat away at your self-worth. To turn this around, create the positive energy you need to promote self-respect.

Since language is a powerful tool, change the words you use to respond to situations by turning your thoughts around. Tell yourself, "I know there are things I need to improve, but there are other areas in which I excel." Other self-esteem boosters can be discovered if you don't overreach but instead set up challenges you can manage, learn to hear and welcome praise, and make a list of your own positive attributes.

21. Find out how superstitious you really are!

"Superstitious beliefs stem from our wish for some outside source of power to keep us protected," says behavioral scientist Donald Dossey, PhD. Take this test to see how superstitious you are and learn how to use it to your advantage.

1. **It's your best friend's wedding day. Which of these do you think it's most important to give her?**

   a. Something old, new, borrowed, or blue

   b. A good-luck hug

   c. A heart-to-heart talk to ease her nerves

2. **If you had to pick a number from one to ten to win a prize, which of these would you choose?**

   a. Seven

   b. Three

   c. Ten

3. **Your favorite kind of book is:**

   a. Science fiction or mystery

   b. Romance or adventure

   c. History or biography

4. **The last time you got an e-mail chain letter promising good luck, you:**

   a. Passed it along

   b. Read it through but didn't pass it along

   c. Got annoyed and deleted it

5. **When you see a full moon, you think:**

   a. That explains all the weird things that have been happening lately.

   b. That's why I've been moody.

   c. Time passes so fast.

6. **Which of these situations would you try to avoid at all costs:**

   a. Walking under a ladder

   b. Breaking a mirror

   c. Misplacing your keys

7. **If your horoscope suggested you avoid making important decisions today, you would:**

   a. Put them off until tomorrow

   b. Ponder those decisions a little more carefully

   c. Ignore it

8. **When you pass a fountain where it's good luck to toss in a coin, you are most likely to:**

   a. Make a wish and toss a coin

   b. Pitch in a penny if you can find one

   c. Try to calculate how much money was tossed in

9. **You just put a bid on the house of your dreams. You:**

   a. Keep it a secret

   b. Tell your best friend but ask her to keep it quiet

   c. Tell everyone how excited you are

10. **When filling out a lottery ticket you use "lucky" numbers or dates:**

    a. Always

    b. Sometimes

    c. Never

According to a CBS-TV poll, one in five Americans say they have seen a ghost!

Your Score

MOSTLY A'S:

You love your superstitions.

"Folks who hold tightly to superstitious thinking believe it could help them avoid everything from daily snags to potential disasters," says Donald Dossey, PhD, author of *Holiday Folklore, Phobias*, and Fun. But superstitious thinking can also be a way to take you out of the driver's seat. Here's how to keep the steering wheel firmly in your hands:

- Write down all the pros and cons before making important decisions, to help you feel more confident about your choices.

- Breathe in courage. Take ten deep breaths to fill your body with calming energy.

MOSTLY B'S:

You've got a few superstitions.

"It's only when life takes unexpected twists that you tend to rely on superstitions to explain it," says Dossey. But you can stay level headed. Just:

- Get a little more sleep. According to the American Sleep Foundation, 70 percent of us could use more sleep and the benefits it provides—such as sharp thinking and high energy.

- Try some positive influences. Whether it's calling a pal or booking a massage, make sure you indulge in whatever brings you joy.

Just the facts for you.

Practical and analytical, you opt for real-world solutions to problems. "But everyone needs a little mystery in their lives," says Dossey. To open yourself up to it:

- Keep a dream diary. Look back thirty days later and see if your dreams offered clues to where you are now.

- Connect with nature to help you appreciate the magic in your life.

22. Are you susceptible to spring fever?

Scientists have discovered the cause of spring fever: light! "Spring's extra light gives some people more energy and optimism," says Lyn Lamberg, coauthor of *The Body Clock Guide to Better Health*.

1. **Most mornings, I'm:**

   a. Grumpy until I fully wake up

   b. Okay, but it takes me about an hour before I feel really alert

   c. Full of energy

2. **When you feel yourself slipping into a midafternoon slump, you seek an energy boost from:**

   a. A ten-minute catnap

   b. Getting up and stretching

   c. Eating chocolate or other sugary snacks

3. **When the days start getting shorter in autumn, you:**

   a. Look forward to the nip in the air

   b. Don't really notice

   c. Feel sad to see summer go

4. **Of these, the holiday you like best is:**

   a. Christmas

   b. Thanksgiving

   c. Fourth of July

5. **As a rule, you are most energetic:**

   a. Around six p.m.

   b. At noon

   c. Before noon

6. **Of these, which color appeals to you most?**
    a. Purple
    b. Yellow
    c. Green

7. **You love the feel of:**
    a. Cozy cashmere
    b. Delicate satin
    c. Crisp linen

Your Score

MOSTLY A'S:

You're immune to spring fever.

The seasons may come and go, but you remain even keeled. "Your body chemistry is not sensitive to the up-and-down effect of light on the brain," explains Lamberg. You have sharp powers of concentration and aren't easily distracted by the environment. You don't suffer feelings of depression or weight gain during the winter, either. But if you want to get a seasonal boost from spring's light-enhancing benefits, experts advise:

- Sleeping with the blinds open to let daylight awaken you naturally. This slow introduction to morning will train your brain to be more susceptible to light's energizing effects.

- Stepping outside as soon as possible after waking up. Exposure to morning daylight can make you alert earlier.

MOSTLY B'S:

You've got a mild case of spring fever.

With spring's extra light, you get a little lift thanks to the boost in the feel-good brain chemical serotonin, and "you feel an appetite for stimulating projects," says Lamberg. "But your initial surge of spring fever tends to sputter before long." To keep that enthusiasm going, Lamberg suggests:

- Resetting your body clock by getting up thirty minutes earlier each day—even on weekends. You'll be awake for prime daylight hours and maximize the benefits of serotonin.

- Keeping your sunglasses off when the sun isn't *too* bright so the full effect of the light's rays will enter your brain.

MOSTLY C'S:

You're highly susceptible to spring fever.

When the first robin appears, you experience the classic signs of spring fever: restless energy, amorous feelings, even the desire to clean! "Your highly sensitive pineal gland keys in to the increase in sunshine, rushing to reverse the winter slowdown," says Lamberg. If you want those edgy symptoms to ease up, try:

- Cutting down on caffeine. Soothing drinks, such as decaffeinated herbal teas, have a calming effect.

- Increasing outdoor activity. The best remedy for spring fever is giving your body what it craves.

23. Tune in to the strongest aspect of your personality!

Turn the radio up—because the kind of music you're listening to holds some amazing clues to who you are. "It's true: music affects our brain even more than language does. That's why a person's music preference reveals key aspects of her personality," explains Howard Brofsky, PhD, coauthor of *The Art of Listening: Developing Musical Perception*. So take note of your choice and discover what really makes your heart sing! If you prefer:

BROADWAY SHOW TUNES:
You're an extrovert.

"Folks who enjoy belting out famous show tunes and often-sung standards in the shower are creative, outgoing, and enjoy being in the spotlight," says Brofsky. Whether you're dancing center stage at a party or just making a presentation at work, you project a stunning combination of confidence and energy that leaves a lasting impression. And you're on the A-list of every hostess in town because you make others feel just as great as you do.

TOP-40 POP:
You're a mover and a shaker!

Think Madonna has energy? She pales next to you! Whether you're cleaning the house or working out, odds are you're doing it to the bouncing beat of today's pop music. "Top-40 lovers are on the move and involved with what's happening around them," says Brofsky. Bothered by litter? You spearhead a neighborhood trash cleanup day! Your new toaster doesn't work as promised? You fire off a letter to the manufacturer! Your can-do attitude and boundless enthusiasm have put you on the fast track to success—and there's no stopping you now!

ROCK 'N' ROLL OLDIES OR CLASSIC ROCK:
You're steady and reliable.

If you look back fondly on a gentler time, you're not alone. "Those who hold onto the music they grew up with also hold onto the solid family values they learned in childhood," says Brofsky. Rock solid and steady, you're the one friends and family come to when they need sensible advice. They know that in the same way you tune out the loud, pounding rhythms of newer music, you also ignore the flimsy advice that sometimes passes for common sense these days, preferring to rely on the tried-and-true values that have come through for you for decades.

COUNTRY-WESTERN:
You're all heart.

"Folks who listen to country-western tunes are compassionate realists who put love, loyalty, and family first," says Brofsky. A self-confessed "softie," you try to make the world a better place: you buy gifts for loved ones for no reason, donate to charity often, and always give others a second chance. This straight-from-the-heart approach to life means you may get hurt more easily and more deeply than others do, but you can weather any emotional storm because you feel the power of love.

CLASSICAL OR JAZZ:

You're an ace problem-solver.

"Those who enjoy classical or jazz music are thoughtful, logical folks," says Brofsky. You're a smart problem-solver. That's why your family calls you when the computer crashes or they need help making clever cutbacks in the household budget. And although you love the quiet company of close friends, you've also got the ability to appreciate your own company—and what could be more useful than that?

LIGHT POP OR EASY LISTENING:

You're stress-proof.

Prefer soothing but upbeat tunes? Odds are your life is jam-packed—but you never feel overwhelmed. "Listeners who gravitate to this type of calming music usually have a lot of things they need to get done, but also have the remarkable ability to tune out distractions," says Brofsky. "They want music that won't upset their concentration." So, whether you're rushing off to an early-morning meeting or hurrying to clean up a dirty kitchen before company arrives, you sail through your day practically stress-free! What's your secret? You focus on the task at hand and let nothing stand in the way of accomplishing it.

24. Are you a leader or a follower?

Do you forge new paths or do you let the flock determine where you're going? See if you've got the stuff to set the pace.

Part One

1. **Your women's club is going on a tour of Istanbul. The very idea of Turkish food makes you whirl like a dervish. You:**

   a. Buy a ticket and pack at least a year's supply of antacid

   b. Are you talking to me? There's no way I would even consider belonging to a women's club!

   c. Suggest a different locale. If they don't bite, beg off.

2. **When you read a list of the most popular television shows, you are usually:**

   a. Flabbergasted. You don't watch any of those mentioned.

   b. Mildly surprised that a few of your favorites are on the top five.

   c. Convinced that the Nielsen ratings are based on you—since you're in total agreement.

3. **You shop for most of your clothes at:**

   a. Big department stores that carry all the name brands

b. Out-of-the-way boutiques

c. Rummage sales, thrift shops, and retro clothing stores

4. Dust off the family photo album and flip through its pages. In the majority of shots, you are:

a. Not there. I was either taking the picture or wandering off.

b. Candidly embracing family members and close friends

c. Striking a pose, looking totally out of place and very embarrassed

5. Which of these special holiday events is your favorite?

a. The Fourth of July. I love a parade!

b. Gift giving around the Christmas tree. It's a great way to show appreciation!

c. Thanksgiving dinner. I get great enjoyment from family gatherings.

6. In the past several elections, the candidates you have voted for:

a. Usually won or ran a close second

b. All won by big majorities

c. Lost, lost, lost!

7. When choosing a brand-new hairstyle, you:

a. Look through the latest magazines to see what celebrities and models are wearing

b. Sketch one on paper and tell your hairdresser to follow your instructions

c. Talk it over with your friends

8. You are happiest in a job when you are:

a. Running your own company

b. Setting your own schedule and feeling the competitive edge

c. Given a daily set of supervised tasks

Part Two

1. Though I may not win any popularity contests, I always have to have my say.

Agree _____ Disagree _____

2. Friends often ask me where I get my clothes.

Agree _____ Disagree _____

3. As a kid, I never wanted to join the Girl Scouts.

Agree _____ Disagree _____

4. I don't see why I should wait for a man to call me when I can just as easily phone him!

Agree _____ Disagree _____

5. Who can be bothered with reading and following recipes? I make up my own!

Agree_____ Disagree _____

Your Score

For Part One, give yourself the following number of points for each answer:

1. a-3, b-7, c-5	5. a-3, b-7, c-5
2. a-7, b-5, c-3	6. a-5, b-3, c-7
3. a-3, b-5, c-7	7. a-3, b-7, c-5
4. a-7, b-3, c-5	8. a-7, b-5, c-3

For Part Two, give yourself 3 points for each statement with which you agree.
Add the scores from Parts One and Two.

39 POINTS OR LESS:
What you crave most out of life is popularity, and you believe the only way to win is to join the crowd. Even when you truly don't agree with the majority, you follow in their footsteps. You're never the first to take a stand or give an opinion. Unfortunately, this attitude is unlikely

to get you far. Stifling the natural urge to share your voice can cause headaches, exhaustion, a weakened immune system, and depression. Stop sitting in the backseat! Once you take the steering wheel, your journey to happiness will begin. Trust your true voice and it will be a smooth ride.

40 TO 55 POINTS:
Generally reserved, you're most comfortable when you fit in with the crowd. Conservative clothes, understated accessories, a preference for popular forms of entertainment, and family harmony are your usual choices. However, when it comes to politics, your children's education, and community affairs, you take a somewhat independent stand and are willing

to take action, even if it goes against popular opinion. Because you're articulate and compassionate, others often follow your lead. Bringing social change brings out the best in you.

56 POINTS OR MORE:
Dynamic and charismatic, it's only natural that you should strike up the band and lead the parade. You're a take-charge person and a dramatic orator who can rally support and draw others into your circle. Whether it's being one step ahead of the latest fashions or chairing committees, you're always making the first move. But there is a catch: you sometimes find yourself unable to conform, even when that might be the best course of action. Remember, a wise person also knows when it's time to follow.

25. What if you won a million dollars?

We all know winning a million dollars can change a person's life—but not always in the way you'd think! How might you be affected? "The answer reveals how you deal with sudden change," says Lynn Cutts, PhD, author of *Change One Habit, Change Your Life*.

1. **You would rather strike it rich by:**
    a. Winning in a casino
    b. Entering a contest or inventing something fabulous
    c. Playing your lucky number in the lottery

2. **If you won a million dollars, the first thing you'd do is:**
    a. Buy that dream house or car you've had your eye on
    b. Give money or gifts to loved ones

    c. Invest the money so you could live off the interest

3. **After your million-dollar check arrived, you'd probably:**
    a. Quit your job and not work for as long as possible
    b. Scale back your job to spend more time with family and on hobbies
    c. Start your dream business

4. **If you played the lottery, you'd:**

   a. Pick whatever numbers popped into your head

   b. Play family birthdays and special numbers

   c. Let the computer choose your numbers

5. **Your dream vacation is:**

   a. A tour of Europe or Asia

   b. A cross-country tour of America

   c. A stay at a tropical island resort

6. **You're suddenly rich and swamped with request for donations. You:**

   a. Pick one favorite charity and writing a big, fat check

   b. Set up a foundation like "Oprah's Angel Network" so others can contribute as well

   c. Make anonymous donations to several charities

7. **Of these, your favorite game show is:**

   a. *Deal or No Deal*

   b. *Family Feud*

   c. *Jeopardy!*

Bill Gates is still the richest man in the United States although he has given away $28 billion!

Your Score

MOSTLY A'S:

You would be a shining star.

A natural extrovert, you would bask under fame and fortune's bright lights and use this attention—and extra time—to make your every wish come true! "You love life and know how to find joy in everything," says Cutts. "Money would just kick that up a notch." And that means also making a big difference in the world around you.

MOSTLY B'S:

You would share the wealth.

Generous by nature, if you won big, you'd most likely be the Oprah of your world, bringing loved ones along to share the bounty and investing in all kinds of community-improvement projects. Never one to forget a kindness, you'd be sure to acknowledge anyone who has helped you and treat them to an extravagant thank-you.

MOSTLY C'S:

You would savor your privacy.

If you struck it rich, odds are you'd steer clear of any spotlight and keep hush-hush about your good fortune. "Comfortable out of the limelight, you'd probably get great satisfaction working behind the scenes, donating to a charity anonymously or funding pet projects without seeking credit," says Cutts. "For you, just knowing you can make a difference would be the greatest reward of all.

26. Find the success secret in your morning routine!

"Everything we do in the morning reveals secrets about how we manage our lives," says Neil Fiore, PhD, author of *The Now Habit*.

1. Before leaving the house you:

a. Casually straighten the bed

b. Leave the bed unmade

c. Make sure the bed is perfectly made

2. Your favorite breakfast is:

a. Nothing, maybe a cup of coffee

b. A hearty sit-down breakfast of eggs and bacon, or cereal

c. A bagel, muffin, or yogurt

3. Awakening after a vivid dream you're likely to:

a. Think about it for a few minutes when you wake up, then let it go

b. Review it in your mind throughout the day

c. Write it down

4. You get the day's weather report from:

a. A morning show like *Good Morning America* or *Today*

b. Your car radio on the way to work

c. Your computer or the Weather Channel

5. On average, it takes you how long to get out the door in the morning?

a. About an hour

b. More than an hour

c. Less than an hour

6. When choosing your wardrobe for the day, you:

a. Pick something quickly and stick with it

b. Try on several things until you find something that feels right

c. Put on the clothes you've selected the night before

7. Your makeup routine includes:

a. A swipe of lipstick and blush and not much else

b. Nothing—you don't wear makeup

c. Everything from foundation to eye makeup

Your Score

MOSTLY A'S:

You're a go-getter.

Your morning is geared toward getting you out the door fast so you can attend to your goals for the day. That means no time for fussing over clothes or makeup, and forget about other distractions—even figuring out last night's dream won't sidetrack you from today's to-do list. "Your ability to prioritize is what makes you so successful," says Fiore.

MOSTLY B'S:

You're highly intuitive.

Your morning routine varies depending on what is going on in your life—from your mood to your ever-changing schedule. Highly sensitive, you're affected by everything from the day's weather to a dream you had. "That's why you follow your intuition in the morning, nurturing yourself with a comforting breakfast and clothes that make you feel good," says Fiore.

MOSTLY C'S:

You're a high-achieving planner.

Everything about your razor-sharp morning routine says you're a brilliant multitasker who knows how to set and stick to a schedule. That's because to you, time is precious. You want to save it for the things—and people—that really matter. Your gift for planning ahead keeps your busy life running smoothly.

27. Which awards extravaganza is your favorite?

Roll out the red carpet, break out the popcorn, turn on the television—and learn something new about yourself. That's right! The one awards show you wouldn't miss for the world reveals things about your personality. Why? "Since each show is unique—from the way the stars dress to the tone, entertainment, sets, and speeches—the one you're most tuned in to reflects how you approach the world," says celebrity-watcher Melissa Rivers. So choose your must-see awards bash and discover why the winner is...you!

THE PEOPLE'S CHOICE AWARDS:

You're a clearheaded problem-solver.

These honors are handed out based on votes from Americans like you. "Folks who tune in to watch tend to be logical thinkers who are confident that their ideas make a difference," says Rivers. Your feisty determination and direct approach to problems indicate "emotional intelligence"—which studies show leads to a happy, successful life!

THE GOLDEN GLOBES:
You're a charismatic dynamo!

"The Golden Globes are known as Hollywood's biggest party of the year, where stars celebrate, schmooze, socialize, and make merry. So if this is your favorite show, you're a gal who really knows how to have a rollicking good time!" says Rivers. A charismatic dynamo, you attract the goodwill of others whether you're on the dance floor, making a crucial presentation at work, or just chatting with the checkout clerk at the supermarket. Drawn in by your fun-loving spirit, chums new and old say you're one of their favorite people—and it's no secret why: you make others feel just as happy as you are!

THE ACADEMY AWARDS:
You're a high achiever.

"Winning an Oscar is the ultimate honor...and if you just love to watch it happen, you aren't afraid to strive for everything life has to offer!" says Rivers. Confident in your abilities and eager to show the world what you can do, you always go for the gusto, whether you're applying for a promotion, searching for a new home, or dressing to the nines for your high school reunion. And you almost always hit your mark! Your secret? Positive thinking. So let your spirit soar because, for you, the sky's the limit!

THE GRAMMYS:
You're a youthful free spirit.

Love the quirky, anything-goes attitude of this hip awards show? "Grammy enthusiasts are usually free spirits who follow their own inspiration and are always up for adventure," says Rivers. Whether you're slicking on the hippest, hottest lip gloss, signing up for a rollerblading class, or moving to the bouncing beat of today's music, you jump into new experiences with both feet! And it's this attitude that keeps you young. Those who stay on top of new developments actually age the least! So turn the radio up, because no matter what the tempo, you're tuned in to the exciting beat of life.

THE TONYS:
You love the limelight.

"Those who are entranced by the spontaneity of the Tonys (the Oscars of live theater) tend to be confident extroverts who love to 'perform' in their own lives," says Rivers. No shrinking violet, you blossom when all eyes are on you and you get the chance to show what you can do. In fact, scientists have found that folks like you have more of a certain brain chemical that makes you crave the limelight—so play to your strength: try signing up for community theater! Who knows? Maybe someday you'll be up there accepting a Tony yourself!

THE EMMYS:
You're a wonderful friend.

The gang from sitcoms, weekly drama series, the hosts of game shows, even news anchors are so familiar to us that we sometimes feel as if they are our pals. "That's why the Emmys have an intimate feel to them. They're a low-key show where you can root for you friends!" says Rivers. Big hearted and compassionate, you take joy in making your loved ones happy, matched only by the love you get in return—and that's a win-win situation for everyone!

28. Discover your memory-boosting style!

"The best way to boost your memory is by using a technique that matches your learning style," says Corinne Gediman, author of *Brainfit*. Take this test to understand how your mind works, and find out which technique for powering up your memory suits you best.

1. **When choosing a paint color for your bedroom, you first:**
   a. Compare lots of paint swatches
   b. Consult with friends or an expert at the store
   c. Paint a few samples on the wall

2. **Lost? The best way for you to find your way back is to:**
   a. Recall landmarks you saw along the way
   b. Call someone for directions
   c. Trace your way back on a map

3. **If you were assembling a child's toy, you'd most likely:**
   a. Read the directions carefully first
   b. Ask someone to read the directions to you while you assemble it
   c. Not bother with directions and put it together by instinct

4. **When bored, you're most likely to:**
   a. Daydream
   b. Hum or doodle
   c. Fidget

5. **Your number one criterion in choosing an alarm clock is:**
   a. The numbers are clearly displayed
   b. The sound is pleasing
   c. It can be set easily

6. **You'd rather spend a free hour:**
   a. Reading
   b. Listening to music
   c. Working on a craft project

7. **You would rather learn a new dance step by:**
   a. Watching a demonstration
   b. Having someone describe the steps
   c. Getting out on the dance floor and just doing it

During their lifetime, most people find it hard to go beyond memorizing 300,000 facts.

Your Score

MOSTLY A'S:

Your memory style is VISUAL.

Like 63 percent of all people, you're a visual thinker who learns by seeing. You have the type of mind that prefers to watch a demonstration before you do it yourself. "When visual learners want to remember something," says Gediman, "they should turn it into a picture." If you want to remember you're parked in row eight, for example, envision the figure eight in your mind.

MOSTLY B'S:

Your memory style is AUDITORY.

Odds are, you prefer hearing books on tape over reading them, and pay more attention to what's being said than done. It's because you're among the 30 percent of the population who are auditory learners, retaining and recalling what you know by ear. To remember something important, Gediman advises, "repeat it out loud."

MOSTLY C'S:

Your memory style is PHYSICAL.

Do you get the urge to touch things and feel their textures? Are you good at hands-on tasks? Chances are you join the 7 percent of us who are "kinesthetically" inclined—which means you learn best by doing and using your sense of touch. So, the next time you want to remember something, write it down. The act of writing will cement it into your memory

29. What's your best time of day?

"We each have a unique, built-in body clock, and discovering when yours peaks will help you maximize every minute of your day," says Lynne Lamberg, coauthor of *The Body Clock Guide to Better Health.*

1. **The time of day you most want a snack is:**

   a. Before eleven a.m.

   b. Around two in the afternoon

   c. After three p.m.

2. **You'd love to see your favorite celebrity interviewed by:**

   a. Regis and Kelly

   b. Oprah

   c. Larry King

3. **How much coffee do you usually drink?**

   a. A cup or less

   b. Two cups

   c. Three or more cups

4. **You typically wake up and:**

   a. Jump out of bed in a good mood and ready to tackle the day

   b. Slowly stretch, easing yourself into the new day

   c. Feel a little grumpy—you're not a fan of mornings

5. **The meal you look forward to most is:**

   a. Breakfast

   b. Lunch

   c. Dinner

6. **By the time the evening rolls around, you're:**

   a. Eager for dinner so you can relax and unwind

   b. Ready to phone friends and catch up on a few chores

   c. Looking forward to a night on the town

Your Score

MOSTLY A'S:

You reach your peak before noon.

No snooze button for you. When your alarm clock goes off, you leap out of bed! Your mental and physical energy percolates in the early-morning hours. That makes you a rare breed—studies show that only 10 percent of us are early birds. "The morning is your best time to tackle a challenge or whiz through your to-do list," says Lamberg.

MOSTLY B'S:

You shine in the afternoon.

Like most Americans, you prefer to rise between seven and eight a.m. and tuck yourself in around eleven at night. That means you usually get a full eight hours of sleep, and that keeps you on an even keel all day long. But you really come alive in the early afternoon, getting a surge of energy that makes this the best time for starting new projects or brainstorming ideas.

MOSTLY C'S:

You sparkle at night.

A natural night owl, you start hitting your stride when the sun begins to set. You get the most accomplished when you stay late at the office, because after five p.m. your energy soars and there's nothing your mind can't handle. Procrastinating actually works in your favor: the later you tackle complicated tasks, the easier they seem to you.

Unfortunately, there's no quick fix for jet lag. What's the best strategy for overcoming it quickly? Set your clock to the local time ASAP and sleep and eat according to the time zone you're in.

30. Can you resist temptation?

Do you have a will or iron—or of wobbly gelatin? Test your strength as we play devil's advocate.

Part One

1. **Imagine this: You are out jogging and George Clooney's double races to your side. He asks you out and, as luck would have it, your man is away on a business trip. You:**

   a. Stop in your tracks and give this handsome hunk your number

   b. Dash off in your Reeboks before your knees go weak

   c. Wipe the sweat from your forehead; tell him he's sweet, but confess that you're taken

2. **You get five pounds of Swiss chocolates for your birthday. One week later, how many are still in the box?**

   a. Most of them. I limit myself to one or two a day.

   b. What's another word for none?

   c. I'm not counting—probably about half.

3. **You discover a wallet filled with cash in the ladies' room of a restaurant. There's no identification. You:**

   a. Take it to the maître d'

   b. Think "finders keepers…," and put it in your purse

   c. Take it home and then run an ad in the local paper

4. **You would consider cheating on your man if…**

   a. Tom Cruise promised to take you to Tahiti.

   b. Never!

   c. Your next-door neighbor made a pass.

5. **It's spring! The sky is blue, the birds are singing—and your house is a mess! You:**

   a. Roll up your sleeves and start washing the windows

   b. Walk out the door

   c. Devote half the day to dusting, the rest to frolicking

6. **Everything is half-price at your favorite boutique, but your bank balance says you're broke. What do you tell yourself?**

   a. With these bargains, if I buy now and pay later, I'll end up saving.

   b. I'd better just keep on walking and not buy a thing.

   c. I'll treat myself to one item—but that's it.

7. **Which statement best reflects your feelings about physical attraction?**

   a. It can be turned on and off like a faucet.

   b. It's pure, uncontrollable magnetism.

   c. It requires careful cultivation.

8. **The clock says midnight and you have to be up early, yet you're in the middle of watching a terrific thriller on television. You:**

   a. Reset your alarm for an hour later and stay up

   b. Watch until the next commercial and record the rest for another time

   c. Reach for the remote and press the "off" button

Part Two

1. **We're in control of our own destiny.**

   Agree _____ Disagree _____

2. **New Year's resolutions are a waste of time.**

   Agree _____ Disagree _____

3. **Willpower is the key to success.**

   Agree _____ Disagree _____

4. **I carry a shopping list to the supermarket and stick to it.**

   Agree _____ Disagree _____

5. **There really can be too much of a good thing.**

   Agree _____ Disagree _____

Your Score

For Part One, give yourself the following number of points for each answer:

1. a-7, b-5, c-3	5. a-3, b-7, c-5
2. a-3, b-7, c-5	6. a-7, b-3, c-5
3. a-3, b-7, c-5	7. a-3, b-7, c-5
4. a-5, b-3, c-7	8. a-7, b-5, c-3

For Part Two, give yourself 3 points for each statement with which you agree.
Add your scores from Parts One and Two.

39 POINTS OR LESS:
Everything excites you and attracts your interest, which means that you're easily distracted. For you, life is a bowl of cherries and you want to taste them all! Lovers find your enthusiasm enthralling, and you easily charm them off their feet. But no sooner do they swoon than you're off walking in the sunset with someone else. For you, the early stages of infatuation are irresistible. Discipline may not be your strong suit, but at least you wear your spontaneity with pizzazz.

40 TO 55 POINTS:
Mastering your own destiny is one of your first priorities, and you try to keep your train on track. But sometimes you derail, usually for good reason. Because you're sensitive to opportunity when it knocks, you're flexible enough to change your plans. However, you're not easily swayed. You manage to achieve an admirable balance between spontaneity and responsibility. You're in complete control, but you know when it's time to let loose.

56 POINTS OR MORE:
You have as much willpower as Arnold Schwarzenegger has muscles. There's no bait strong enough to lure you away from your designated plans. A maven at making lists and schedules, organization is always your goal. Temptation would never think of crossing your path. Those who choose you as a friend or lover are bound to find you faithful and reliable. You're not likely to fall in love at first sight, but, after extremely careful scrutiny, you will hand over your heart—forever.

31. What's your Chinese element?

"According to ancient Chinese medicine, every personality can be matched to a natural element: water, fire, earth, wood, or metal," says Laurie Steelsmith, author of *Natural Choices for Women's Health*. What's yours? Read on!

1. **Your doctor prescribes light exercise. You decide to try:**
   a. Yoga
   b. Swimming
   c. Bicycling
   d. Dancing
   e. Walking

2. **Choose one of these colors to paint your bedroom walls:**
   a. Blue
   b. Red
   c. Green
   d. Gold
   e. Lavender

3. **Deciding on a screensaver? You'd opt for:**
   a. A nature scene
   b. A scene from a popular TV show or movie
   c. A picture of a family member or pet
   d. A famous masterpiece
   e. Anything that's personally meaningful to you

4. **Choose the actress whose looks you most admire:**
   a. Jennifer Anniston
   b. Catherine Zeta-Jones
   c. Meg Ryan
   d. Jane Seymour
   e. Nicole Kidman

5. **Your favorite thirst quencher is:**
   a. Water
   b. Iced coffee or tea
   c. Juice
   d. Vitamin- or flavor-enriched water
   e. Soda

6. **Of these, the gemstone you like most is:**
   a. Aquamarine
   b. Ruby
   c. Emerald
   d. Diamond
   e. Sapphire

7. **If you were home alone on a rainy day, you'd:**
   a. Relax
   b. Invite friends over
   c. Catch up on chores
   d. Write in your journal or read
   e. Watch TV

YOUR SCORE

MOSTLY A'S:
Water.

Like the ocean, you possess a quiet strength. Your confidence comes from a knack for diplomacy and ability to lead by example. "Generally serene, you let your instincts be your guide," says Steelsmith.

MOSTLY B'S:
Fire.

"Fire types are born leaders who burn with intensity," says Steelsmith. And your magnetic personality draws others to you. Bold and competitive, you thrive on new adventures.

MOSTLY C'S:
Earth.

"Earth types are more logical than emotional. If something makes sense, you do it, if not, you move on," says Steelsmith. A hard worker, you prefer taking life slowly and enjoying the gifts around you.

MOSTLY D'S:
Metal.

Like the firmness of metal, you know what you want and stand your ground in getting it. "You also like to get the most from life and that includes a desire for luxury, comfort and freedom," says Steelsmith.

MOSTLY E'S:
Wood.

You're naturally open minded, with a deep sense of empathy. Like a tree, you're solid in your principles, but at the same time, "You're receptive to learning what others might teach," says Steelsmith.

32. Do you need more privacy?

Part One

1. **I often feel I have to wake up early to get a jump on the day.**

   a. True

   b. False

2. **My partner frequently opens the mail before I get to it.**

   a. True

   b. False

3. **If I think I'm about to cry, I try to leave the room.**

   a. True

   b. False

4. **I find it hard to say no.**

   a. True

   b. False

5. **My children often interrupt me when I'm having a conversation.**

   a. True

   b. False

6. **My usual "time-out" is a minute or two with my eyes closed.**

   a. True

   b. False

Part Two

7. **You're soaking in a warm tub when the phone rings. You:**

   a. Climb out and answer it

   b. Let it ring

8. **When struggling with a personal problem, you work through it by:**

   a. Mulling it over with your spouse or friend

   b. Pondering it alone

9. **When you finally get some peace and quiet, you often feel:**

   a. On edge

   b. Fabulous

10. **When it comes to daydreaming, you're a:**

    a. Novice

    b. Champ

11. **You receive a confidential letter from a troubled friend. To make sure no one peeks at it, you keep it:**

    a. Tucked inside a book on your nightstand

    b. In your nightstand

Your Score

MOSTLY A'S:

You're due for some solitude.

Good-natured and responsible, you love helping others—but this same selflessness can leave you feeling depleted. What's the solution? Recharge with some time to yourself. Instead of filling your date book with endless meetings and family functions, set aside one-half hour a day for journal-keeping, reading, or solo strolls. And when someone asks you to give up that personal time, remember the magic word: a polite no!

MOSTLY B'S:

You know when to fly solo.

You have a healthy respect for your own time and how you spend it! Although you enjoy socializing and giving of yourself, you also recognize those times when you need solitude. By pulling away from group activities occasionally, you satisfy a need that almost everyone has: to stay in touch with yourself. And once you return to the action, you're recharged and raring to go!

Studies have shown that people who keep a journal make two-thirds fewer trips to the doctor than those who don't.

33. What does your kitchen say about you?

It's the room where many women spend the most time, so "Each choice you make about it—from the appliances to the walls—offers key insights into your outlook and strengths," says Denise Medved, author of *The Tiny Kitchen*. This quiz reveals what's really cooking in your kitchen!

1. **Your kitchen counters are usually:**

   a. Clean, neat, and uncluttered

   b. Packed with small appliances, knickknacks, even the mail

   c. Adorned with pasta jars, special oils, and other treats

2. **You prefer kitchen walls that are:**

   a. White or a pale shade

   b. Brightly colored

   c. Stenciled or wallpapered

3. **Your pots and pans are:**

   a. Stored neatly in cabinets

   b. Stashed wherever they fit

   c. Hung on a pot rack

4. **You've decorated your kitchen with:**

   a. Carefully coordinated artwork

   b. Flowers—fresh, artificial, and everything in between

   c. Pictures made by your children, your friends' children, or your grandkids

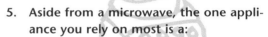

5. **Aside from a microwave, the one appliance you rely on most is a:**

   a. Food processor/mixer

   b. Programmable coffeemaker

   c. Crock Pot

6. **Your ideal kitchen window coverings are:**

   a. Sleek blinds

   b. Simple shades or curtains

   c. Ruffled or floral panels with a matching valance

7. **The kitchen floors you most love are:**

   a. Wood or laminate

   b. Tile

   c. Linoleum

Your Score

MOSTLY A'S:

You're on top of it.

Organized and methodical, your kitchen is always in apple-pie order! Your cabinets boast airtight containers and matching pots and pans, and you've got lots of built-in storage, too. "You're a multitasker who keeps supplies within reach and always stays focused," says Medved. Since you use your time so expertly, you rarely get stressed—even when there are a dozen guests for dinner! What's your sanity-saving secret? You always clean up as you go.

MOSTLY B'S:

You're a creative spirit.

Your kitchen reflects your imagination and enthusiasm. "You're always experimenting with whatever's new, whether it's ultra-modern decor, the latest gadget, or exotic recipes," says Medved. What's more, you know how to improvise with flair! Sometimes your kitchen gets messy, but so what? You've got the spirit of a true artist.

MOSTLY C'S:

You're a nester.

No matter how busy you get or how far away you roam, home is always where your heart is. That's why your kitchen reflects comfort in its homemade accessories and big table where everyone can hang out. "You're definitely more warm, shabby-chic than cool sophisticate," says Medved.

34. What's your most irresistible quality?

"We all have a stand-out quality that draws others to us," says Debbie Mandel, author of *Turn on Your Inner Light*. Take this quiz to discover yours.

1. **Channel surfing during the day, you'll probably stop to watch a:**

   a. Talk show

   b. Soap opera

   c. Movie

2. **You do most of your reading to:**

   a. Get information—news, health tips, and financial advice

   b. Escape—fiction, mysteries, romances

   c. Keep up with scoops—celebrity gossip, fashion tips, recipes

3. **If you were going to change your hairstyle, you'd opt for:**

   a. Something short and sassy, like Jennifer Love Hewitt's

   b. A straight and stylish do, like Jennifer Anniston's

   c. A fun and feminine look, like Kate Hudson's

4. **Your favorite part of planning a party is:**

a. Figuring out the guest list

b. Planning the menu

c. Picking a theme and decorating

5. **Your answering machine's outgoing message is:**

a. Simple and direct

b. Upbeat and happy

c. Amusing

6. **Aside from the darker basics, the majority of your clothes are:**

a. Neutrals

b. Soft pastels

c. Bright colors

7. **Which of these sounds like a fun job?**

a. Secret shopper

b. Tour guide

c. Talent scout

Your Score

MOSTLY A'S:

You're irresistibly CONFIDENT!

Independent and solidly self-assured—that's what others notice most about you. "There's nothing more appealing than being around someone who knows herself and feels in control of her life. It makes others feel more capable and optimistic, too," says Mandel. With your strong sense of self, you believe there's nothing you can't do when you set your mind to it.

MOSTLY B'S:

You're irresistibly WARM!

An attentive listener with a generous and compassionate nature, you go the distance to make people feel welcome in your home and your life. That's what makes you unforgettable. "Since you're a master at reading unspoken cues, you really know what others are feeling— so folks know they're truly being heard and understood," says Mandel.

MOSTLY C'S:

You're irresistibly FUN-LOVING!

Life is never boring when you're around, which is why your friends put you at the top of every invitation list and won't make plans unless they're sure you can attend. Witty, spontaneous, creative, and outgoing, you're the life of the party. "Even in stressful situations, you squeeze in a little fun and make everyone relax," says Mandel.

Big surprise! What's the number-one trait men find most appealing in women? Good looks!

35. What does your favorite flower say about you?

What's the quickest way to alter your mood? Expose yourself to a new color or scent. "Color and scent are the two most powerful stimuli in the natural world, and when they're combined—as nature does in flowers and trees—their power to affect us gets even stronger," says Ellen Dugan, author of *Garden Witchery*. That's why the spring flower you favor most speaks volumes about your basic needs. Here's what it means if you like…

TULIPS:
You're a gutsy go-getter.

Tulips are the least delicate of spring flowers. Planted in autumn, they grow underground all winter and burst forth with hardy stems and petals. "Folks who are drawn to tulips are go-getter types who have little time for frills," says Dugan. You cut right to the chase, saying what you mean. Did you propose to your husband instead of the other way around? Are you the first one to speak out and voice your opinion? Absolutely! Your gutsiness makes you a force to be reckoned with.

DAISIES:
You're a chameleon.

"People who prefer daisies over other flowers have most likely reinvented themselves by changing their careers or looks, or starting over with a new marriage or even a blank slate," says Dugan. Daisies represent change and possibility: chromologists (color experts) would say it's because of their color. White is usually associated with new beginnings. Your motto is, "Tomorrow is a new day," and you welcome the possibilities it will bring.

The most popular flower in the world? The rose!

ROSES:
You love the limelight.

Women who rank roses as their favorite flower are usually confident. "Roses are bold, look-at-me flowers that thrive in bright sunlight. You're drawn to them because you feel the same way about yourself," says Dugan. Have you ever been plucked from an audience onto the stage? Found yourself the center of attention at a party for someone else? Sure—because your charisma makes heads turn your way.

LILACS:

You're compassionate.

Women who rate the scent of lilacs above all else tend to be extremely compassionate. (Not surprisingly, lilacs are the favorite scent of nurses, nationwide!) And compassionate people are emotionally intelligent: they can read the social and psychological cues of others. "You understand what people need," says Dugan, "and that makes you a special wife, mother, and friend."

BUTTERCUPS:

You radiate optimism.

When subjects are shown yellow flowers during object association studies, their mood immediately brightens and the "happiness centers" of their brains light up. Why? "Yellow is the color of sunlight, and scientists say those who respond to it most tend to be the most optimistic—and the most easily cheered," says Dugan. Never one to let a rainy day get you down, you instinctively want to be happy—and you usually manage to find a way to make any situation brighter. Research shows this kind of optimism is contagious. (There's real truth to the saying, "Smile and the world smiles with you.") That's undoubtedly why you're so popular.

36. Can you spot a flea-market bargain?

You know what you like, "but with a few insider secrets, you can also get the best price every time," says G. G. Carbone, author of *How to Make a Fortune with Other People's Junk.*

1. **If you make an offer and the seller pulls on his ear, you:**

   a. Consider offering a higher price to encourage him to say yes

   b. Hold firm to your price

2. **You are more likely to bag a real treasure if you:**

   a. Buy an item you really fall in love with

   b. Are on the lookout for a specific collectible

3. **When dressing for a day of yard-sale shopping, you wear:**

   a. Something nice so the seller will be impressed and assume you know what you're talking about

   b. Comfy sweats

4. **You go to a flea market carrying:**

   a. A mix of big and small bills

   b. Small bills

5. **If there's no price marked on an item, you:**

   a. Ask the price

   b. Suggest a price

6. **You try to bargain down a seller by:**

   a. Mentioning a flaw or two in the item

   b. Being charming and making small talk

7. **You'll get the best deal on a particular piece by:**

   a. Pretending you're not that attached to it

   b. Showing some interest in it

8. **It's best to go flea-market shopping:**

   a. With one dedicated buddy who also loves bargain hunting

   b. With a group of friends

9. **If you like several items at a yard sale, it's best to:**

   a. Ask for a group price

   b. Bargain each one down individually

Your Score

Give yourself 2 points for each correct answer.

1-A. This is the universal cue for "indecision"—and a few more dollars might help him make up his mind.

2-A. Focusing on one category of items and closing off possibilities means you'll be more likely to pass up treasure.

3-b. If a seller sizes you up as someone with a bigger budget, they'll be less inclined to accept a lower offer.

4-B. When sellers are forced to track down change, they have time to reconsider the bargain price they just mentioned.

5-a. Even your lower offer might be higher than what the seller is willing to take. So always ask the price before making an offer.

6-a. You catch more bees with honey, so chat with the seller about how long he's had an item, if he's having a good selling day, etc.

7-b. The seller might have an attachment to the item and will be more likely to reduce the cost if he thinks you share his appreciation for it.

8-a. When it comes to bargain-hunting, you'll be less apt to miss a real find if you shop with one good treasure-seeking buddy.

9-a. Sellers are always happy to get rid of multiple items. And if it's starting to get busy, he'll be even more inclined to make a quick sale.

BETWEEN 14 AND 18 POINTS:

You're a top-flight wheeler-dealer!

Your discerning eye makes you a natural when it comes to bagging the best deals. "You've also mastered the psychological savvy needed to get a seller to take a lower price and you have strategies for zooming in on a treasure," says Carbone. Although you're usually on target, your enthusiasm can sometimes end in costly impulse buys. Instead:

- When in doubt, take ten. Ask the seller to hold an item for ten minutes, so you can consider your purchase. More than 50 percent of the time, consumers change their minds.

- Keep your resources front and center. When dealers see you have a price guide on hand, they know you're an educated buyer—which makes them more likely to give you a better price," says Carbone. Haggling a little helps, too.

You've got some flea-market sense.

You have the instincts to net flea-market bargains, but sometimes your thrifty side wins out over your instincts and you pick useful items over treasures. That's not so bad—but be sure to start with a clear strategy:

- Scope out the scene first. Make a circle around the flea market and then visit only what interests you. You'll feel less overwhelmed.

- Show the seller you're serious. Flash your cash and say, "I'm ready to give you twenty dollars for that right now—it's my best offer."

You're missing the true bargains.

Your enthusiasm may lead you to some wonderful finds—but you tend to gush over them, causing you to spend more than you need to. Here's how to put on your best yard-sale poker face:

- Don't try to negotiate when you're tired. This is the time when you'll be more likely to let your heart overrule your reason.

- Give yourself a budget and carry cash. Don't take your checkbook if it means you'll be tempted to spend more than you can afford.

37. Are you right-brained or left-brained?

Scientists link creativity with the right side of the brain and logic with the left. "Knowing which you favor can help you develop your talents," says Scott Thorpe, PhD, author of *How to Think Like Einstein*. Take this test and find your dominant side.

1. You do your best thinking:

a. Sitting

b. Lying down on a couch

c. Standing or walking

2. Of these, your best subject in high school was:

a. Math or science

b. Music or anything in the arts

c. English or history

3. Your desk is:

a. Neat as a pin

b. Cluttered

c. A little messy, but you know where things are

4. Learning a new dance step? You'll probably learn it faster by:

a. Watching a video that you can stop and start

b. Practicing with a partner who already knows the moves

c. Taking a class

5. **You are:**

   a. Right-handed

   b. Left-handed

   c. Ambidextrous

6. **You're more likely to choose a movie based on:**

   a. Reviews

   b. Coming attractions or commercials

   c. A friend's recommendation

7. **The type of painting you'd most likely hang in your bedroom is:**

   a. An abstract design

   b. A landscape

   c. A portrait

Your Score

MOSTLY A'S:

You're left-brained.

Logical and objective, you work best alone in a quiet environment. "With your analytical mind, you can quickly decipher fact from fiction and find the most practical solution to any problem," says Thorpe. No wonder you're a whiz at numbers, too. You crave order and tend never to be late to anything.

MOSTLY B'S:

You're right-brained.

Intuitive, creative, and sensitive, you see the world through your emotions and solve problems by following your heart. Spontaneity is your strong suit, and you trust your instincts when it comes to first impressions. "Right-brain thinkers are highly social," says Thorpe, "and like to work in groups."

MOSTLY C'S:

You're a little bit of both.

Consider yourself the perfect mix of rationality and creativity. You can tap into either side, depending on the situation. "Highly flexible, you're willing to compromise and you have an easy time changing direction at the last minute," says Thorpe. Although making a decision takes you a while, once you make up your mind, you stick to it.

38. What does your favorite eye color reveal about you?

We've all heard that old saying, "The eyes are the window to the soul," but there may be more truth to it than anyone realized. "A study of more than one thousand women proves that the color of contact lenses we would choose is directly linked to specific personality traits—and that 64 percent of us would love to change our eye color to better match how we want others to view us," reveals Jan Sheehan of FreshLook Cosmetic Lenses. That's why manufacturers have created a rainbow of new contact lens colors that go way beyond what nature gave you. So choose the eye color you dream of wearing—and discover how you really want the world to see you!

EMERALD GREEN:

You want to appear ALLURING.

"Green eyes are seen as signaling good looks and a confident allure. Folks who would love to have them know how to make the most of their natural charisma," says Sheehan. Wonderfully comfortable in your own skin, you feel beautiful and captivating wherever you go, and this magnetism makes friends and admirers fall at your feet. What's your secret? You know that the true essence of popularity is confidence in yourself: If you believe you're attractive, others will too!

HONEY:

You want to appear WARM AND NURTURING.

"Our studies show that honey-colored lens wearers are happiest when they're cast as compassionate 'mom' types," says Sheehan. Honey brown is associated with a strong sense of security and belonging. You love to feel needed and nothing makes you happier than when loved ones come to you for support. And guess what? Nothing makes them happier, either: According to surveys, one of the most important qualities Americans look for in friends and romantic partners is good listening skills.

TURQUOISE:

You want to appear OUTGOING.

For centuries, the color turquoise has been associated with optimism and upbeat energy, and that's why today folks with bright turquoise eyes are generally regarded as outgoing and fun. "Turquoise has the power to boost your mood, which is why blue-green lighting is now being tested as a treatment to counteract depression," says Sheehan. You are a real life-of-the-party type and your bouncy energy and never-say-die attitude see you through good times and bad. You know how to rally the troops and get them smiling. Your good mood is contagious and everyone wants to be around your fun-loving attitude.

BRIGHT SAPPHIRE:

You want to appear FRIENDLY.

One of the most powerful findings uncovered by researchers connecting eye color to personality was that "almost every respondent said that bright, clear, true-blue eyes indicate a friendly, girl-next-door quality," says Sheehan. And if you long for you own set of baby blues, chances are you want the world to see what a wonderful friend you are! Kind and effervescent, you positively bubble over with goodwill. You may not be a cheerleader, but your sweet, gentle spirit makes you just as popular as one.

AMETHYST:

You want to appear MYSTERIOUS.

"Those who long for amethyst eyes want to be seen as enigmatic, spiritual, and creative," says Sheehan. Never one to reveal too much about yourself to those you don't know well, you're a private person who gets great satisfaction from achieving things on your own, without help from teachers or friends—whether you're repainting your bathroom, teaching yourself yoga, or starting a diet plan. No mystery here: your private side gives you the space you need to soar.

SLATE GRAY:

You want to appear SMART.

"In color-association tests, gray is the color of intellect," says Sheehan. Longing to change your look to cool, reflective gray? Then you're most likely a deep, steady thinker with a quiet resourcefulness and quick-witted agility that enables you to perform under pressure. No matter what the crisis, you stay calm when everyone around you is panicking, and you do it with a quiet finesse that always saves the day.

Part Two

Relationships

1. How well do you read body language?

1. **You're telling your husband all about your plans to redecorate and, as you speak, he leans on his elbow with his chin in his hand. You should:**

   a. Keep talking

   b. Decide to share your plans with a friend instead; he's too polite to say so, but he's bored

   c. Ask his opinion; he's got his own ideas to share

2. **"Yes, I've finished my homework, Mom," your daughter tells you, rubbing her nose. Your next question:**

   a. "Are you sure?"

   b. "Are you coming down with a cold?"

   c. "Are you afraid you didn't do a very good job?"

3. **You want the job interviewer to think of you as a confidant. One way to reinforce this is to:**

   a. Initiate a handshake when you meet and leave

   b. Look her in the eye steadily

   c. Walk slowly but deliberately into the room

4. **While you are telling the sales clerk why you want a refund on a blouse that fell apart after two washings, she folds her arms across her chest. You:**

   a. Feel encouraged and continue talking; she's on the defensive, but she's likely to do what you want

   b. Ask to see a supervisor; it's obvious you're getting nowhere with her

   c. Wrap it up; you can tell she's ready to surrender the cash

5. **Your boss of ten years is leaning back in her chair, arms behind her head, as you talk to her. She:**

   a. Wants to gain power or control over the conversation

   b. Feels perfectly relaxed and comfortable with you

   c. Is gearing up to give you bad news

6. **You (and lots of other people) wish your local swimming pool would open earlier or on weekends. To convince the manager, you will:**

   a. Raise your voice slightly on the key points

   b. Use a lot of hand gestures for emphasis

   c. Nod slowly as you speak

Your Score

Give yourself 5 points for each correct answer.

1-b. This gesture shows boredom.

2-a. Nose rubbing often accompanies a fib.

3-c. Initiating a handshake and staring directly at someone can both communicate aggression.

4-b. Crossed arms are a clear signal that someone is closed off to your requests.

85

5-b. In a well-established relationship, this is a relaxed gesture—but in a new one, it can be an expression of power.

6-c. This gesture encourages assent by the listener.

IF YOU SCORED 25 TO 30 POINTS:
You are a brilliant translator.

You pay careful attention to nonverbal clues. As a result, you're often the first one to realize what's going on, and you can adjust your own communication accordingly to make sure everything goes your way!

IF YOU SCORED 15 TO 20 POINTS:
You are an instinctive interpreter.

Although you can't always put your finger on how you know, you understand the feelings and motives behind people's words. To increase your insight, try paying more attention to subtle facial gestures.

IF YOU SCORED 10 POINTS OR LESS:
You are still learning the language.

You're just a beginner now, but it's easy to bone up on body language. You might want to pick up a book on body signals, then observe groups of people from a distance and pay closer attention to those you know.

2. Rate your parenting skills.

Are you a by-the-book mom, one who gives her kids free rein...or do you fall somewhere in the middle? Find out!

1. **If your teenage daughter was so busy that she couldn't join the family for meals on a regular basis, you'd probably:**

   a. Insist she change her schedule

   b. Arrange to have one real family meal on the weekend, perhaps brunch

   c. Allow for her hectic life and try not to make an issue of it

2. **Your four-year-old is afraid there's a bear under her bed. You:**

   a. Explain that bears don't live in houses

   b. Let her join you while you check under the bed, and then leave on a nightlight or lamp

   c. Sit with her until she is able to fall asleep

3. **Your preschooler is unusually shy. Your first instinct is to:**

   a. Push her to come out of her shell

   b. Arrange lots of play dates so she learns to socialize with other children

   c. Relax and give it time; kids usually grow out of shyness

4. **You believe that your teenage son is hanging around with the wrong crowd. You:**

   a. Insist he stay away from them or he'll be grounded for good

   b. Invite the whole group over so you can get to know them before passing judgment

   c. Let him know your feelings without making any threats

5. **Your child wants you to buy a toy you think is just a hunk of junk. You:**

   a. Refuse to buy it, pointing out that it's worthless

   b. Tell her if she really wants it, she can buy it with her own savings

   c. Get it although you know it will probably fall apart before you bring it home

6. **What's your television policy?**

   a. We don't allow television, only specially selected children's DVDs.

   b. We discuss as a family which shows are acceptable in our home.

   c. We leave the viewing to our children's discretion.

7. **Your philosophy of discipline is best described by which of the following?**

   a. We lay down the law; they obey the rules.

   b. When things start getting out of hand we call a time-out so we can take the most sensible course of action.

   c. Kids will be kids; we just hope they'll learn from their mistakes.

Your Score

Give yourself 3 points for each "a" answer, 6 points for each "b," and 9 points for each "c."

IF YOU SCORED 21 TO 33 POINTS:
Your parenting skills could be considered "old school," where children are brought up according to a set of rigid rules. Setting clear boundaries is fine—but understand that kids need a voice, too. Be open to their point of view and make sure they feel they've been heard and their desires considered. If you have discipline problems, find out if your community offers a course in parenting skills.

IF YOU SCORED 34 TO 51 POINTS:
You treat your children with respect and include them in decision-making whenever possible. However, when circumstances require a firm stand, you're willing to take it. Although you never discipline with physical punishment, you often call a time-out to give everyone a chance to cool down and reevaluate the situation.

IF YOU SCORED 52 POINTS OR MORE:
You tend to take a hands-off approach to parenting, sometimes allowing too much freedom. Don't be afraid to set limits and say no when you're certain a situation calls for it. You won't lose your children's love. In fact, in the long run, they will appreciate your guidance.

3. What kind of impression do you make? The secret is in your hair!

Did you know that the way you part your hair tells others a lot about you? "A part sends hidden signals about whether you're using more of your left or right brain—and that determines important traits like how serious, creative, or logical you are," says cultural anthropologist Catherine Walter. So take a peek at your part—and learn what your hair is saying about you.

RIGHT PART:
You're a heartfelt caregiver.

Got a right-sided part? You're driven more by your heart than your head! "Our research has found you have an abundance of intuitive, creative, and nurturing traits, which makes you extremely open and giving," says Walter. The best part of all the giving you do? The love that comes back to you a thousand fold!

CENTER PART:
You're naturally stress-proof.

No one would ever call you a stress junkie! That's because, like your part, you seek out a sense of balance no matter what's going on. "Middle-parters tend to be middle-of-the-road folks with a low-key demeanor, who avoid getting caught up in the fray," says Walter. You rarely get upset when there's a snag and you're apt to take a quick time-out when things heat up. And aren't you wise! Research proves that stress-busters like these lower blood pressure and heart rate to produce instant calm!

NO PART:
You're a creative trailblazer.

"Women with no part (the least popular look) tend to be quirky, interesting, artistic types who dance to their own beat," says Walter. Creative change is what brings you true happiness, and that's good news. A flexible, imaginative mind is an indicator of high intelligence. Whether it's trying a jewelry-making class or rearranging your bedroom furniture, your creativity always takes the lead.

LEFT PART:
You're a reliable go-getter.

Folks who part their hair on the left are left-brain thinkers—logical and detail-oriented. "These are the people with orderly minds focused on reaching goals," says Walter. In fact, surveys show that left-parted folks make great elected officials, probably because they have so many strong opinions.

The most valuable hair ever? Elvis Presley's! His personal barber sold a 3-inch strand for $115,120!

4. What color fuels your relationships?

Experts say that your romantic side has a color all its own, and "knowing it can ensure happier relationships," says psychologist Taylor Hartman, PhD, author of *The Color Code*. Take this quiz and discover yours.

1. **Of these, the stone that appeals to you most is:**
   a. Amethyst or garnet
   b. Opal or moonstone
   c. Tiger eye or topaz

2. **Your favorite bedsheets are:**
   a. Smooth and satiny
   b. Crisp linen or cotton
   c. Warm and cozy flannel

3. **You like chocolate best in the form of:**
   a. A rich slice of gooey cake
   b. A box of assorted bonbons
   c. A double-dipped ice-cream cone

4. **At parties, your favorite thing to do is:**
   a. Mix and mingle with lots of different people
   b. Have an intimate conversation with one interesting person
   c. Dance, dance, dance!

5. **Your idea of the perfect Valentine's Day celebration is:**
   a. Breakfast in bed
   b. A bouquet of long-stemmed roses or a box of chocolates
   c. A night on the town

6. **Which of these romantic comedies would you love to see again?**
   a. *Sabrina*
   b. *When Harry Met Sally*
   c. *My Big Fat Greek Wedding*

7. **You like your pizza with:**
   a. Everything
   b. Extra cheese or no extras at all
   c. Yummy pineapple—Hawaiian style!

Your Score

MOSTLY A'S:
You're a passionate RED.

Fueled by fiery intensity, you run headfirst into romance, holding nothing back. "A take-action gal, you're happy to make the first move," says Hartman. You stoke the flames of affection with plenty of imaginative rendezvous! And you adore the spotlight, which is why you probably have a signature fragrance and lots of head-turning outfits. Your charm and boundless energy make you positively unforgettable!

MOSTLY B'S:
You're a sentimental BLUE.

A sensitive romantic, you have high ideals and put the object of your affection on a pedestal. "You cherish every romantic moment," says Hartman. You're a good listener, too. Thanks to your intuition, you're always there for the one you love. And odds are, your loyalty inspires devotion to you!

MOSTLY C'S:
You're a charismatic YELLOW.

Fun-loving and upbeat, you beam with sparkling enthusiasm and a zest for life! "You love to be praised and in return, generously compliment your partner," says Hartman. Naturally optimistic, you live for today and love adventures. You aren't afraid of taking a romantic risk because you see it as ensuring your own happy ending.

5. Can you keep a secret?

Would you rather walk over burning coals than betray a confidence? Take this test to see how your honor rates.

Part One

1. **Imagine you're at a dinner party. While digging into dessert, you relate a personal story—a steamy tale of passion and romance. Your audience is rapt. You:**

   a. Realize you're hogging the spotlight and change the subject

   b. Relish their interest and embellish the story

   c. Reel in your tale with a simple ending. Then ask if anyone else has had a similar experience.

2. **It's your mate's birthday. You are most likely to:**

   a. Cook his favorite meal

   b. Throw him a surprise party

   c. Buy him new underwear

3. **Speaking of birthdays, when people ask your age, you:**

   a. Tell the truth. Wisdom comes with age.

   b. Remind them a lady never tells.

   c. Cut two years off. You look terrific—why not?

4. **You've gained five pounds and feel like a blimp, but you have to attend a big bash. You wear:**

   a. Your slinky dress, once you've let out the seams

   b. A black dress that you hope will make you look thinner

   c. A tentlike dress that reveals nothing

5. **Dream-job time. Which career is most appropriate for you?**

   a. Spy

   b. Gossip columnist

   c. Politician

6. **Oh, no! You just saw your best friend's husband embracing another woman. You:**

a. Call her immediately and tell everything—it's for her own good

b. Calm down and think things over before saying a word

c. Speak to her husband first

7. **If you noticed your daughter's friend was cheating at Monopoly, you'd:**

a. Overlook it. They're just children.

b. Pull the friend aside and explain the downside of cheating.

c. Wait until she left and tell your daughter her friend doesn't play fair.

8. **You've just won the lottery. What do you do first?**

a. Tell whoever is standing closest to you!

b. Buy your family lots of presents

c. Call your partner—he should be the first to know

Part Two

1. **I believe that when you give your word, it should never be broken.**

Agree __X__ Disagree _____

2. **I would never tell someone the end of a movie.**

Agree __X__ Disagree _____

3. **Little white lies are lies nonetheless.**

Agree _____ Disagree __X__

4. **A politician's personal life is his own business.**

Agree __X__ Disagree _____

5. **If I knew that my co-worker was getting fired, I'd hold my tongue. That kind of news should come from the source.**

Agree __X__ Disagree _____

Your Score

Part One: Give yourself the following number of points for each answer:

1. a-5, b-3, c-7	5. a-7, b-5, c-3
2. a-5, b-7, c-3	6. a-3, b-7, c-5
3. a-3, b-5, c-7	7. a-7, b-3, c-5
4. a-7, b-5, c-3	8. a-3, b-7, c-5

Part Two: Give yourself 3 points for each statement with which you agreed.
Add your scores from Parts One and Two.

39 POINTS OR LESS:
Because you're open and honest, keeping a secret is not one of your greatest talents. In fact, if you found someone's (anyone's!) diary, you'd probably share its contents with the world. Here's some advice: Before blabbing anyone's secret, ask yourself, Is it better left unsaid? You'll be surprised how frequently your inner voice will answer in the affirmative. Although truth-telling is admirable and your candor refreshing, this doesn't necessarily make you trustworthy. In your case, honesty isn't always the best policy.

40 TO 55 POINTS
"Let your conscience be your guide," is the motto you follow. Although you hate to fudge the truth, when a matter is hush-hush, you try to avoid spilling the beans. Although you have, on rare occasions, let some juicy gossip slip out, on the whole you're the soul of discretion, and that's probably why so many friends share their secrets with you. Openhearted and above board, you are a loyal friend and a true-blue lover.

56 POINTS OR MORE:
A woman of mystery, you keep your life a closed book. If there are skeletons in anyone's closet (including your own), they stay put. You guard the secrets in your care. And because you respect people's privacy, you are completely dependable— wild horses couldn't drag even a whisper from your buttoned lips. You would probably make a terrific therapist or lawyer—but—I wonder…might there be times when revealing what you know is the best course of action in the long run? It is worth some consideration.

6. Do you think too much?

Research shows that 52 percent of women mull things over and over before making a move. "But thinking too much can trap the brain in a 'worry' cycle," explains psychologist Susan Nolen-Hoeksema, PhD. Break the cycle midthought with this quiz!

1. **After an argument is resolved, do you find yourself still going over your position in your mind?**
   a. Never
   b. Sometimes
   c. Often

2. **When you think back on recent conversations, how often do you wish you'd said something else?**
   a. Rarely
   b. Sometimes
   c. Often

3. **Which method do you most often use when making a decision?**
   a. I go with my gut.
   b. I weigh the pros and cons.
   c. I try to leave my options open.

4. **How often do you check the radio or television for news?**
   a. Maybe once a day
   b. In the morning and evening
   c. Hourly, if possible—but at least a few times a day

5. **How well do you concentrate while learning new tasks?**
   a. I have great concentration.
   b. I concentrate fairly well.
   c. I have a lot of trouble concentrating.

6. **Last time you wanted to change your hair color, you:**
   a. Just did it
   b. Asked a few friends and loved ones what they thought
   c. Practically took a national poll—and still wasn't sure

7. **When it's time to buy your best friend a birthday gift, you:**
   a. Know in your heart what she would like
   b. Shop around until you find something that seems right
   c. Ask her what she really wants

8. **When making plans for the day, you tend to:**

   a. Go with the flow

   b. Make a list and try to stick to it

   c. Reprioritize throughout the day and often reconsider plans

Your Score

MOSTLY A'S:
You make decisions easily.

Once you make a decision, you move right on. That's because, most of the time, you perform the "four essential steps of an action-taker," according to Nolen-Hoeksema:

1. Sorting through challenges
2. Grasping complexities
3. Staying focused
4. Envisioning a positive outcome

It's great that you are comfortable making decisions, but keep in mind that sometimes snap decisions can be wrong. Reduce the possibility of making a rash choice by:

- Sleeping on it. Research shows we can actually problem-solve in our sleep and awaken with the best solution.

- Getting a second opinion. You're used to going it alone, but the old adage "Two heads are better than one" is a good mantra for you.

MOSTLY B'S:
You sometimes think too much.

Since women are raised to be heart centered, it's not uncommon for you to second-guess yourself and others. But this can bog you down. To break the cycle:

- Look for distractions. When you begin over thinking, get up and change places. Studies show that a new vantage point can be enough to shake you out of a fruit-less thought process.

- Keep a handwritten stop sign on your desk. Visual cues can cut down on excessive thinking.

MOSTLY C'S:
You're an overthinker.

Because you are a perfectionist, small concerns can avalanche into big problems—and then letting go is virtually impossible. "You're often flooded with worries that swirl around and around in your mind, making it difficult for you to resolve problems," says Nolen-Hoeksema. But you can halt overthinking. Here's how:

- Envision a happy ending. Praying or meditating on a positive outcome will block negative thoughts.

- Steer clear of "worry buddies," friends who tend to overthink things just as you do. Reaching out to a positive thinker will help you think positively, too!

7. What's your communication style?

"Knowing your personal style of communicating can help you rally people effectively," promises Carmine Gallo, author of *10 Simple Secrets of the World's Greatest Business Communicators*.

1. **Which of these are you more likely to wear around your neck?**
   a. A chunky beaded necklace
   b. A classic string of pearls
   c. A charm or locket with sentimental value

2. **When you have to make a speech or presentation, you:**
   a. Rehearse in front of a mirror
   b. Run it by friends
   c. Quietly read your notes

3. **Pick the "Desperate Housewife" you think is the most honest:**
   a. Lynette
   b. Bree
   c. Susan

4. **Your favorite hot drink is:**
   a. Coffee—the stronger the better
   b. It varies—cider, latte, chai…whatever strikes your fancy
   c. Tea

5. **Which of these stars is your dream guy?**
   a. Harrison Ford
   b. George Clooney
   c. Tom Hanks

6. **If a friend moves away, you are most likely stay in contact via:**
   a. Phone
   b. E-mail
   c. Cards and gifts

7. **Of these, the job in which you would shine most is:**
   a. Entrepreneur
   b. Politician
   c. Actor or artist

Your Score

MOSTLY A'S:

You're a straight talker.

A no-nonsense type who says and does exactly what she means, you keep things simple and direct. "You speak your mind without embellishing the facts," says Gallo. Brimming with confidence, you keep your conversations short and sweet and never fidget when delivering difficult news.

MOSTLY B'S:

You're a seasoned diplomat.

Flexible and fair, you size up your audience before speaking, carefully choosing your words to inspire rather than ruffle any feathers. "Since you can see both sides, your balanced view keeps you neutral even in sticky situations," says Gallo. No wonder you make friends easily and keep them for life.

MOSTLY C'S:

You speak from your heart.

When you talk, you always look people in the eye and punctuate your words with a gentle touch on the arm. "You really listen and gauge how others respond to what you're saying by watching their body language," says Gallo. That's why family and friends come to you for compassionate, nonjudgmental advice.

8. Do you try too hard to please?

If you're like most women, you go out of your way to make sure your loved ones are happy—even if that means stretching yourself too thin. "Women are 80 percent more likely than men to try too hard to please those around them, and they feel guilty when they can't," says Jana Kemp, author of *No! How One Simple Word Can Transform Your Life*. Take this quiz to see if you try too hard—and get tips for letting yourself off the hook.

1. **It is extremely important to be liked by everybody.**
   a. Not necessarily
   b. Usually
   c. Always

2. **I go out of my way to avoid confrontation.**
   a. Not necessarily
   b. Usually
   c. Always

3. **I often hear myself saying "I should have" or "I ought to."**
   a. Not necessarily
   b. Usually
   c. Always

4. **I'd rather criticize myself than blame others.**
   a. Not necessarily
   b. Usually
   c. Always

5. **I often keep my real feelings to myself.**
   a. Not necessarily
   b. Usually
   c. Always

6. **At a party, I'm more likely to help the hostess than relax and socialize.**
   a. Not necessarily
   b. Usually
   c. Always

7. **I find it difficult to delegate.**
   a. Not necessarily
   b. Usually
   c. Always

8. **Compliments make me uncomfortable.**
   a. Not necessarily
   b. Usually
   c. Always

9. I apologize even when I'm right, just to keep the peace.
   a. Not necessarily
   b. Usually
   c. Always

10. I frequently have headaches.
   a. Not necessarily
   b. Usually
   c. Always

Your Score

Give yourself 1 point for every "a" answer, 2 points for every "b," and 3 points for every "c."

IF YOU SCORED 10 TO 15 POINTS:
You have no trouble saying no!

With a schedule you stick to like glue, you stay focused on your priorities! Confident and assertive, you value boundaries in your personal life—which is why you can just as easily say no as yes. "Balanced types like you experience less work-family conflict and can keep stress at bay because you set up strategies for juggling your many roles," says Kemp. But your Type A personality means you have a hard time being flexible. To increase your flexibility:

- Wait 24 hours before giving an answer to something you're not sure about. "Sleeping on it" helps clarify priorities.

- Find an easy solution. Instead of volunteering precious time to a charitable cause, make a donation just this once. Or, instead of baking cookies for the church bake sale, buy them.

- Try to temper or qualify your responses. Phrases like "When I can" or "Maybe in the future" will show you're open to a possibility but not locked in.

IF YOU SCORED 16 TO 20 POINTS:
You're a great juggler.

You can make everyone happy and still manage to find time for yourself. What's your secret for stress-free people-pleasing? "Your strong sense of self allows you to follow your gut reaction and set priorities with guilt-free confidence," says Kemp. But even the best jugglers face the occasional balancing act. When it happens:

- Delegate. If you can't do something, suggest or enlist someone else who can. This way you can stay involved without having to take full responsibility.

- Optimize. When you're at home, turn off your cell phone, laptop, beeper, and e-mail so that you can be fully present for your family.

IF YOU SCORED 21 TO 30 POINTS:
You're the ultimate crowd-pleaser!

Ever wonder why you give and give? Scientists say it's in your brain! For 60 percent of women, the emotional right side of their brain—the part that affects relationship-building—is highly developed. Here are some proven ways to overcome the endless yes cycle:

- Practice saying no to little things, even if it's just to your reflection in the mirror first. This can give you the confidence to make it a habit.

- Reward yourself once in a while with stress-free activities, such as reading or watching a video. You'll feel more relaxed and learn to put yourself first once in a while.

9. What's your social style? There's a clue in the way you hold your drink!

Body language speaks volumes about our personalities, and a new study shows that the way we grasp our glass at a social event can be a clue to who we are. "Since drinking is both essential to survival and a common social activity, the way you hold your glass reflects your strongest socializing traits," explains Patti Wood, author of *Body Language and First Impressions*. Here's what it means if…

YOU HOLD YOUR GLASS TILTED INWARD NEAR YOUR CHIN, WITH YOUR ELBOW TUCKED IN AND THE GLASS PRESSED TO YOUR LIPS:

You're a smooth talker.

Tactful and diplomatic even in the stickiest situations, you negotiate your way around life's rough spots. Two of your guests aren't speaking? You make a light quip to defuse the tension. A co-worker's new hairdo is a hair-don't? You compliment her on her pretty blouse to make her feel better. While others may get frustrated, you're always able to come up with the perfect, friction-defusing response.

YOU HOLD YOUR GLASS FIRMLY IN THE MIDDLE WITH ONE HAND WHILE GESTURING WITH THE OTHER:

You're a charismatic dynamo.

"Holding your glass firmly indicates that you're extremely self-confident," says Wood, "while bold conversational gestures with the other hand shows you're no shrinking violet." Your take-charge, can-do attitude and outgoing, charismatic personality attract others to you like a moth to a flame—and that's great because you're happiest when you're center stage. Whether you're making a fashion statement by wearing a daring accessory, chairing a PTA committee for an important new cause, or starring in the latest community theatre production, you love the limelight. But you're sensitive enough to know when it's time to step back and let others shine—and that's what true charisma is all about.

YOU STARE QUIETLY INTO YOUR CUP, CRADLING IT WITH BOTH HANDS:

You're an etiquette expert.

You were always taught to mind your manners and you've learned the lesson well. Never one to be loud or brash, you keep a polite low profile that speaks volumes about your refined, old-fashioned elegance. "Your genteel manner is fueled by your desire to make a good impression on those you meet—which you accomplish not by rocking the boat but by slowly charming the people inside it," says Wood.

YOU PLAY WITH YOUR GLASS, RUNNING YOUR FINGER AROUND THE RIM:

You're a creative genius.

Quick: Do you like to redecorate your home? Make homemade holiday ornaments? Chances are, you said yes. Your creativity and originality know no bounds. "Inspiration comes to you constantly," says Wood. "You look at every object—even a drinking glass—and see its playful potential." Whether you know it or not, you've probably impressed the boss recently with your original solution to a problem, and you also impress your kids or younger siblings with your unique, young-at-heart ideas for fun.

YOU HOLD YOUR GLASS ALOFT BECAUSE YOU MAKE FREQUENT TOASTS:
You're a real people pleaser.

"Miss Congeniality, you get your energy—and lots of pleasure—from helping and pleasing others," says Wood. At a party, you're almost always the one who starts a toast because it makes you feel good to make others feel good. And that's what makes you so popular. Whether you're offering to drive your daughter and her

friends to the movies, inviting new a co-worker out to lunch to help her feel more comfortable, or cooking up your husband's favorite dinner as a special surprise, you get a warm glow knowing that you've made someone's day.

10. What makes you so magnetic?

Ever wonder why people are drawn to you? "Everyone has a special quality that attracts others to us," says relationship expert Jill Spiegel, author of *Pocket Pep Talk*. "Knowing what yours is can help you open more doors at work or in your personal life." Take this quiz to discover your personal draw.

1. **Research shows that the way we sleep reflects how we carry ourselves while awake. You tend to sleep:**

   a. Curled up on one side

   b. On your back or stomach

   c. In a variety of positions

2. **If you were planning a girls' night out, you'd choose:**

   a. Dinner at an intimate restaurant

   b. A movie or a comedy club

   c. A field trip to a nearby city where you could paint the town red

3. **You'd prefer a birthday party that's:**

   a. A small gathering of your closest friends

   b. A big bash at home with lots of friends, family, and acquaintances

   c. A lavish surprise party at a nice restaurant

4. **Studies show a link between favorite comfort foods and personality traits. Of these, your favorite feel-good food is:**

   a. Homemade chicken soup

   b. Pizza

   c. Ice cream

5. **If you found a kitten outside your door, you'd probably:**

   a. Bring her in and adopt her

   b. Take her to a shelter or vet to make sure she's healthy

   c. Keep her while posting "found" signs around the neighborhood

6. **You feel most comfortable giving advice based on:**

   a. Your personal experiences

   b. Information you've read

   c. Your instincts

7. **When you have a quick question for a friend, you prefer to:**

   a. Talk to her in person

   b. Call her on the phone

   c. Dash off an e-mail

Your Score

MOSTLY A'S:

Your magnetism comes from GENUINE COMPASSION.

"People are drawn to you for your empathy and kindness," says Spiegel. With you, they feel understood and special, as though they're the only person in the room. It doesn't take long for you to make a connection with everyone you meet. Your calm and steady presence makes those around you feel safe and strong.

MOSTLY B'S:

Your magnetism comes from INTELLIGENCE AND WIT.

"Thanks to your curiosity and sense of humor, you instantly engage those around you and spark their creativity," says Spiegel. You look at ordinary situations in surprising ways, read everything in sight, and are always full of interesting facts. It's no wonder people come to you for up-to-the-minute advice: you expand their horizons, too!

MOSTLY C'S:

Your magnetism comes from ENERGY AND ENTHUSIASM.

You've got a zest for life that's positively contagious! "Studies show that energetic people increase the optimism and confidence of those around them," says Spiegel. Your can-do attitude can boost sagging morale and offer that extra push to get things moving. Friends, family, and co-workers love to bask in your bright, "nothing's impossible" attitude.

11. What would your pet say about you?

1. **You're busy watching television when your cat suddenly appears and rubs her furry self against your legs. You:**

   a. Stroke her and ask, "What's wrong, honey?"

   b. Engage her in a game of dangling thread

2. **You're serving steak for dinner and you can picture your dog's "what about me?" gaze already, so you:**

   a. Fix him a small piece

   b. Save your scraps

3. **When going on a family vacation, you're more likely to:**

   a. Get a pet-loving friend to house-sit

   b. Find a motel that accepts pets

4. **It's raining but your puppy is telling you that nature calls. You:**

   a. Hold an umbrella over Fido as you walk him

   b. Let him have fun scampering through the raindrops and puddles

5. **Your dog has a litter of pups. Which would you be most tempted to keep?**

   a. The sweetest and shyest

   b. The feistiest

6. **You're more likely to keep your cat entertained with:**

   a. An engrossing videotape of a fishbowl

   b. A catnip-filled ball

Forty-four percent of us carry pictures of our pets in our wallets!

7. **When you see a fellow dog owner on the street, you usually:**

   a. Say hello but keep walking. You have to keep the pooches apart to prevent a tussle.

   b. Stop to chat and let the dogs get acquainted

8. **Your pet sleeps in:**

   a. Her own cozy bed

   b. Your bed

9. **If you were taking a family portrait, would you include your pet?**

   a. Probably not.

   b. Of course! He's a member of the family.

10. **You reward you pet most often with:**

    a. Kisses and hugs

    b. Yummy treats

Your Score

Note: If your score falls equally between the two categories, read both descriptions, since you share characteristics of both types.

MOSTLY A'S:

You're a NURTURER.

Your pet knows you're naturally protective and loving and that your number one priority is to make sure she's happy, healthy, and safe. You understand her moods and often consider her needs over your own. "Thank you for taking such great care of me," she would say if she could talk. "I sure am lucky!"

MOSTLY B'S:

You're a REAL PAL.

Warm and affectionate, you have a knack for making your pet feel really special. He truly appreciates the way you take him everywhere, spend hours playing, and buy him great toys and treats. Above all, he cherishes the fun you have together.

12. What's your coping style?

We all have an inborn mechanism that helps us manage challenges. "Tuning in to key personality traits such as the ability to look at the big picture, take advice, and be patient, can help you overcome obstacles," says life coach Christine Hassler author of *A Woman's Guide to Balance and Direction*. Take this quiz to see whether you're inspired by a challenge. Then get tips on how to make the most of what comes naturally to you.

1. **If a colleague were out sick and your boss put her work on your desk, you would:**
   a. Do only what you could comfortably take on
   b. Take care of it all, even if it meant staying late

2. **The kind of vacation you like most is:**
   a. A lazy, relaxed holiday at a beach retreat
   b. A trip to a new place where there's lots to do and see

3. **If your best friend offered to fix dinner, you would be more likely to:**
   a. Relax and enjoy the fruits of her labor
   b. Express your appreciation and offer to pitch in

4. **When you meet new people, you're more focused on:**
   a. Getting to know them
   b. Making a good impression

5. **You find evenings are a great time to:**
   a. Curl up in front of the television
   b. Catch up on your bill paying and phone calls to friends

6. **The last time you were stuck in a traffic jam you:**
   a. Tuned in to some relaxing music and just kept inching your way along
   b. Turned on the traffic report and continually switched lanes in an attempt to move more quickly

7. **When you make a mistake you think:**

   a. What can I learn from this?

   b. How can I correct it?

8. **I sometimes forget my watch.**

   a. True

   b. False

9. **I enjoy sleeping late.**

   a. True

   b. False

10. **While in the express lane at the supermarket, I never count the items in the cart ahead of me.**

    a. True

    b. False

11. **I make time to visit my close friends frequently.**

    a. True

    b. False

12. **It's easy for me to ask for help.**

    a. True

    b. False

Your Score

Give yourself 10 points for each "a" answer and 5 points for each "b."

BETWEEN 80 AND 120 POINTS:
You're naturally easygoing.

You can let problems and projects flow in and out of your life while staying calm and collected because your immediate reaction is not to control, fix, or change them. Instead, "You process situations slowly, asking a lot of questions and weighing the pros and cons before coming to a conclusion," says Hassler. You also ask for support if you need it. Psychological studies on happiness show that this approach will lead you to make decisions that are best for you. The downside is that others may view you as passive—and in some cases you do take a backseat. After you gather all the facts, here's how to be more proactive:

- Ask yourself "How am I really feeling?" Let yourself experience negative emotions. "Naturally easygoing people have a tendency to sugar coat or repress their authentic reaction," says Hassler.

- Make a list of actions or goals you need to reach and then give yourself a deadline to achieve them. Take actions step by step so you don't feel overwhelmed.

- Become a leader. If you're coping with a situation that involves other people, trust yourself to be at the helm. Calm types like you can diffuse or mediate a situation effectively because you don't get emotionally charged.

BETWEEN 55 AND 75 POINTS:
You're inspired by stress.

Whatever the task, you're determined to do it quickly and perfectly, leaving no stone unturned. "I can't" is just not in your vocabulary. "This type of personality is actually turned on by difficulty and inspired by challenge," says Hassler. "In fact, when there's a job to be done you go the extra mile to make sure it's done just right!" Being an overachiever is admirable, but you may find yourself bored with routine—even creating extra work for yourself just to keep life interesting. What's more, since you want everything to go perfectly, it might be difficult to let go of control. With so many logs in the fire, you run the risk of burning out—so aim for balance. Here's how:

- Schedule pleasurable activities. Stress junkies have a hard time sitting still, so recharge by making stress-free but fun dates with friends and family.

- Delegate. Trust others who have expertise to carry some of the load. "If you're feeling insecure, it's okay to check in once in a while," says Hassler.

- Open your palms. Surprisingly, a study shows that this simple "letting go" gesture actually helps release the impulse to take over.

50 POINTS OR LESS:
You're sometimes over-whelmed.

"Scoring within this range means you tend to react to situations emotionally and often feel a little anxious—especially when new situations present themselves," says Hassler. You might have had a recent disappointment that makes you wary of new situations. Add to the mix your busy schedule, trying to balance work, family, and social responsibilities—and who wouldn't feel overwhelmed? No wonder you look for quick fixes! You don't have the time (or so you think) to dig deeper and come up with a more grounded approach. To avoid feeling overwhelmed, try these coping techniques:

- Get the emotion out first. Let yourself cry or yell. You might try a kick boxing class, writing in a journal, or viewing a comedy for a hearty belly laugh. "As long as you get the emotion out first," says Hassler, "the stress level will be reduced."

- Go on a "mind vacation" and allow your decision to evolve. Window shop, take a walk, just loll around at home. "Studies show we do our best problem-solving subconsciously. Just by giving yourself time before taking action, your decisions will evolve from reactionary (or emotionally-charged) to intuitive," Hassler says.

- Take action without expectation. Try not to label your decisions or work either a success or a failure. This approach will help you continue to move along towards your goal without self-criticism.

- Check out again. Allow yourself to take another break if you start to feel overwhelmed. Signs of stress include a headache, muscle tension, nail biting, jaw clenching, and difficulty breathing.

A brief hug and ten minutes of handholding with a romantic partner greatly reduces the harmful physical effects of stress, according to a study conducted by the School of Medicine at the University of North Carolina–Chapel Hill.

13. What kind of mom are you?

Your family adores you and you take great care of them, but what traits make you stand out as a mom? "Every mother has something that makes her unique, and knowing where you shine will help you maximize your parenting skills," says Susan Fletcher PhD, author of *Parenting in the Smart Zone*. Take our test and discover your personal mom power!

1. **When your child is having a tough time with homework, you:**
   a. Sit beside her, making yourself available for questions
   b. Suggest she do what she can and then let her teacher know what she found too difficult
   c. Offer your help unconditionally

2. **If your toddler is having a tough time falling asleep even though it's past his bedtime, you:**
   a. Stay with him silently in his room until he falls asleep
   b. Allow him to stay up for another fifteen minutes
   c. Read him a story or sing a soft lullaby

3. **You tend to decide what to make for dinner by:**
   a. Choosing from among your children's favorites
   b. Asking what everyone wants and then going with the majority
   c. Making different dishes to suit each taste

4. **Your seventeen-year-old insists she wants a butterfly tattoo on her ankle. You:**
   a. Open a discussion of the pros and cons
   b. Ask her to wait another month before coming to a decision
   c. Go with her to make sure it's a safe procedure

5. **When it comes to chores, you:**
   a. Do them together!
   b. Make completing them a condition of your children's allowance
   c. Give the kids a reward when they're done!

6. **You would rather spend a day with the kids:**
   a. Playing outdoors
   b. Doing whatever they're in the mood for
   c. Lounging around the house—no pressure

7. **The most important value to instill in your child is:**
   a. Confidence
   b. Respect
   c. Compassion

8. **Which of these classic toys would you opt to buy for a five-year-old?**

   a. Puzzle

   b. Cards

   c. Bubbles

9. **The classic TV mom you most resemble is:**

   a. June Cleaver

   b. Carol Brady

   c. Donna Reed

10. **Every mom gets stretched to her limit once in a while. What do you usually do to calm your nerves?**

    a. Breathe deeply and count to ten

    b. Make a real effort to see your kids' side

    c. Take five and leave the room for a few minutes

Your Score

MOSTLY A'S:
Your power is in your PATIENCE.

With the patience of a saint and the ability to stay focused and attentive, you know how to wait until you catch your child doing something right and then compliment her, reinforcing positive behavior. Fletcher says patient moms like you also "Use words carefully and calmly, and always thinking before speaking." Plus, you rate high on the frustration tolerance scale—so when plans need to change unexpectedly, you stay cool and collected. Your kids learn from your example: they're flexible, willing to take positive risks, and know how to remain confident and cool under any condition.

MOSTLY B'S:
Your power is in your FAIRNESS.

You never keep score, hold a grudge, or compare your children to anyone else's. You see the big picture, don't get hung up on unimportant details, know how to weigh the pros and cons, and look at both sides of any situation. "The ability to be fair comes from your willingness to stay open and listen to your kids without judgment," says Fletcher. You don't need to push your personal agenda! Your balanced approach to parenting creates mutual respect and will lead your children to become independent and creative adults.

MOSTLY C'S:
Your power is in your GENTLENESS.

Ever wonder why everyone wants one of your hugs, and the kids in the neighborhood all want to hang out at your house? It's because your sweet and loving nature creates a comforting and soothing environment. "Gentle moms like you possess high levels of empathy—and everyone feels it, especially your kids," says Fletcher. That's why they know they can talk to you about anything! Plus, you never overschedule or put too much pressure on them. So, even in this high-intensity, competitive world, your children know that when you're around they can just relax.

Here are some additional ways to be the best mom you can be:

- Make time just for you! When you take time for yourself, you increase your patience and reduce stress, making you an even better mom!

- Keep the kids busy! Create an activities bag packed with crayons, pencils, books, papers, and puzzles. Leave the bag by the door and take it with you when you take the kids out for chores or appointments.

- Be consistent. Child psychologists say it's the best way to ensure that your children will take what you say seriously. This in turn will help them grow into secure and confident adults!

- Forgive yourself! Realize that no mother is perfect 100 percent of the time. When your kids see that you can forgive yourself, they'll learn that it's okay to make mistakes sometimes, as long as we learn from them.

14. How popular are you?

There are four key traits that popular people tend to possess: listening skills, empathy, flexibility, and generosity. "The more of these you have, the higher your popularity quotient, and the more likely people will flock to you," says Laurie Puhn, author of *Instant Persuasion*. Figure out your popularity quotient—and then learn some easy ways to give it a boost.

1. **Which statement do you agree with most?**
   a. I am supportive of my friends, even when they are wrong.
   b. I'm loyal, but I don't hide my real opinions.

2. **At work, you're generally:**
   a. Open to a give-and-take collaboration
   b. More comfortable taking the lead

3. **You typically:**
   a. Trust your first impressions about people
   b. Take your time to form an opinion about someone

4. **Your plans are usually:**
   a. Flexible and open to change
   b. Firm and goal oriented

5. **Which is more of a problem for you?**
   a. Your desire to help others means that you often can't say no.
   b. You get stressed out if you don't have a little quiet time.

6. **When your plans change suddenly, you usually:**
   a. Go with the flow
   b. Get a little flustered

7. **When listening to someone else, you almost always make eye contact:**
   a. True
   b. False

8. **You always remember people's names:**
   a. True
   b. False

9. **You pay attention to posture.**
   a. True
   b. False

10. **You laugh easily at jokes.**
    a. True
    b. False

Your Score

Give yourself 7 points for every "a" answer and 3 points for every "b."

IF YOU SCORED 56 TO 70 POINTS:
You've got popularity plus!

"People want to be around you because when they are, they feel good about themselves," says Puhn. Happy when your friends succeed, comforting when they're in need, you listen and respond from the heart. What's the rub? Since you attract such a wide circle of friends, you may not have enough time for you. To avoid popularity burnout:

- Listen to your inner voice. If you feel stress from overcommitment, simply say no, and trust that friends will still like you just the same.

- Make an appointment with yourself. Studies show that solitary time devoted to reflection and relaxation energizes you by easing anxiety and even lowering your blood pressure by up to 10 percent.

- Step back from friends' difficulties once in a while. Listen, but remind yourself, "I can't solve everyone's problems."

IF YOU SCORED 40 TO 55 POINTS:
You're selective.

Forget about having hoards of people around—you prefer a small, close-knit group of pals. Slightly shy, you form deep and lasting relationships based on two essential traits: generosity and empathy. Empathy is essential for forming meaningful friendships—but if you feel the desire to widen your social circle:

- Join groups that share your interests, such as a reading group or even a poker game.

- Suggest that your close friends introduce you to their acquaintances.

- Strengthen your conversational skills by chatting with people when you're in line at the market, post office, or movies.

IF YOU SCORED 30 TO 39 POINTS:
You run your own race!

A strong-minded individualist who prefers to go it alone, you have the perfect skills to be a high-powered manager. "But being a leader doesn't always translate to popularity," says Puhn. Here's how to connect more:

- Before you offer advice, ask if it's wanted. It could be that your friend just needs an ear.

- Create a good first impression. Make eye contact, remember names, ask questions, and listen. Research shows that within ten minutes of meeting someone, he or she forms an opinion about you, and these things can make it a good one.

- Ask yourself: "How would I feel?" It's the best way to practice empathy, an important popularity trait.

15. Are you a good judge of character?

1. **Have you ever trusted someone, only to be disappointed?**

   a. No

   b. Yes

2. **You and a friend finally find time to meet for lunch and she seems rather cool. You are more likely to:**

   a. Ask her what's up

   b. Listen carefully for clues to her mood

3. **Two of your co-workers are whispering when you pass by. You are likely to think:**

   a. Aha! Plans are underway for the boss's surprise party!

   b. Hmmm…maybe some interesting news will be coming my way later.

4. **Do you believe in love at first sight?**

   a. No.

   b. Yes.

5. **An acquaintance has begun sharing very personal information with you. You are more likely to:**

   a. Reciprocate in kind

   b. Share some stories of your own, but not deeply personal ones

6. **You're in the market for your first home and a real estate ad describes one as a "cozy charmer." You're more likely to:**

   a. Figure this means it's probably small

   b. Call the agent for details

7. **Before deciding which movie to rent, you:**

   a. Look at the cast; your favorite actors rarely let you down

   b. Check through the movie reviews in your paper for one with at least a three-star rating

8. **How often do you guess "whodunit"?**

   a. Quite often

   b. Occasionally

9. **A recently divorced friend suddenly gets a total makeover: new clothes, new hair color, the works! You are more likely to:**

   a. Assume she's feeling better about her life

   b. Ask her if she's found someone special

More than 50 percent of us believe in love at first sight!

Your Score

Note: If your score falls equally between the two categories, read both descriptions since you share characteristics with both.

MOSTLY A'S:
You size people up.

You're exceptionally intuitive and your tools for navigating life are your on-target gut feelings. Sensitive to others' body language and vocal inflections, you're attuned to the subtle clues that reveal the true nature of someone's character and the truth of a complex situation, saving you from many a mistake.

MOSTLY B'S:
You trust your experience.

Patient and confident, your motto is, "Time will tell." Believing that you learn something every day, your calm approach has saved you from judging hastily and inaccurately. You always give friends and co-workers the benefit of the doubt.

16. What makes you a great friend?

"Each of us offers our friends a unique ingredient that cements the relationship," says sociologist, B. J. Gallagher, author of *Friends Are Everything*. This test shows why your friends love you!

1. **If you won a thousand dollars, you'd be more likely to:**

   a. Invest it

   b. Spend just a little, but save most of it

   c. Treat yourself and loved ones to anything you want!

2. **The celebrity best friends you most admire are:**

   a. Matt Damon and Ben Affleck

   b. Courtney Cox and Jennifer Aniston

   c. Penelope Cruz and Salma Hayek

3. **If a friend asks you for fashion advice for a big night out, you:**

   a. Tell her to opt for classics, like a little black dress

   b. Compliment her taste and suggest a few special pieces from her wardrobe

   c. Offer lots of tips for accessories that dress up just about any outfit!

4. **If your close friend were planning to drive cross-country, you'd**

   a. Wrap up an atlas with a big bow

   b. Give her a travel journal and pen

   c. Take her out for a farewell dinner

5. **If a friend had the flu, you'd bring her:**

   a. A natural remedy such as vitamin C or echinacea

   b. A pot of homemade chicken soup

   c. A funny video or stack of magazines

6. **Your favorite way to spend an evening with friends is:**

   a. Going out for dinner and girl talk

   b. Having everyone over to your house for dinner and a DVD

   c. Getting dressed up and painting the town red

7. **If your best friend got her dream job, you'd:**

   a. Buy her a beautiful day planner to get her started off right

   b. Make her a big gift basket with special pampering treats

   c. Plan a surprise party to celebrate!

Your Score

MOSTLY A'S:

Your friends count on YOUR GREAT ADVICE.

Straightforward, thoughtful and insightful, you're the first person your friends turn to when they need some wisdom. You intuitively have the most practical suggestions and creative alternatives. "Good advice-givers like you avoid preaching and can simply size up a situation to come up with the best solution," says Gallagher.

MOSTLY B'S:

Your friends count on YOUR COMPASSIONATE SHOULDER.

One of the most valued traits in a friend is the ability to be a good listener—and you're tops on that score! Naturally empathetic, you hear with your heart first and understand what your friends feel instinctively. "Authentic listening tells your friend that she is important to you, that her problems are legitimate, and that you care deeply about her," says Gallagher.

MOSTLY C'S:

Your friends count on YOUR FUN-LOVING NATURE.

You're the type who can instantly turn lemons into lemonade and whip up an outing that melts away stress. Optimistic and upbeat, you think life is too short to focus on the downside of anything. "Laughter is a guaranteed stress-buster," says Gallagher. Your ability to bring joy to your friends puts you at the top of their A-list!

17. How forgiving are you?

Someone's done you wrong! Do you string 'em up or let 'em off the hook? Quiz yourself and see if mercy's in your makeup.

Part One

1. **If your mate arrived thirty minutes late for dinner, what would you do first?**
   a. Give him a look that could kill
   b. Ask what happened
   c. Demand you eat out

2. **At the supermarket, the checkout clerk is as slow as molasses. You:**
   a. Figure she must be tired and offer to help pack your own groceries
   b. Complain to the person in front of you
   c. Tell the clerk to hurry up!

3. **If someone gives a speech filled with flubs, you think:**
   a. Everyone makes mistakes.
   b. How did this guy ever get where he is?
   c. He's feeling the pressure.

4. **When your good friend forgets your birthday, you:**
   a. Purposely let her birthday go by without saying a word
   b. Forgive and forget
   c. Tell her

5. **Your son trades his $300 bicycle for a $30 video game. You say:**
   a. "Well, it's your mistake."
   b. "Get your bike back now before I blow a gasket!"
   c. "Guess you'll have to save up for your next set of wheels!"

6. **Your dog leaves a mess on your sofa again. You:**
   a. See if any of your more relaxed friends are interested in adopting your pooch
   b. Clean it up. These things happen.
   c. Call a dog trainer

7. **As you are turning the corner, a neighbor pulls out of her driveway and plows into your car. You:**
   a. Blow off steam in her direction, then exchange insurance information
   b. Embrace, and thank the heavens no one was hurt
   c. Sue!

8. **You lock yourself out of the house. You think:**
   a. I'm so careless. I should be locked up permanently!
   b. Big deal. This could happen to anyone.
   c. I'll never leave the house again without checking my purse for the keys first.

Part Two

1. **Even when I feel wronged, I try to look beyond the hurt.**

   Agree _____ Disagree _____

2. **We're only human and bound to make mistakes.**

   Agree _____ Disagree _____

3. **I rarely, if ever, hold a grudge.**

   Agree _____ Disagree _____

4. **If my man cheated on me once, I'd give him a second chance.**

   Agree _____ Disagree _____

5. **Friends tell me their deepest, darkest secrets.**

   Agree _____ Disagree _____

Your Score

For Part One, give yourself the following number of points for each answer:

1. a-5, b-7, c-3	5. a-5, b-3, c-7
2. a-7, b-3, c-5	6. a-3, b-5, c-7
3. a-7, b-3, c-5	7. a-5, b-7, c-3
4. a-3, b-7, c-5	8. a-3, b-7, c-5

For Part Two, give yourself 3 points for each statement with which you agree.
Add the scores from Parts One and Two.

39 POINTS OR LESS:

When you feel wronged, you're merciless. In fact, no matter how sincerely an apology is offered, you're apt to ignore the gesture. Sometimes, depending on the seriousness of the offense, you might even resolve to get even. But there may be a reason for your hard heart; as a child you were probably given the same severe treatment. Now you cherish a grudge as if it were a valuable gem. But forgiveness may be the balm that heals your old wounds, so it's time to open your heart. The next time you feel slighted, turn the other cheek; this one act of compassion will put a smile on your face—and may be the beginning of a more forgiving you.

40 TO 55 POINTS:

You rarely take offense at others' transgressions and you tend to let bygones be bygones. Resentment is just not a feeling you frequently experience; rather, compassion is your key trait. You're not a saint, though, so some things do get under your skin. You're a stickler for honesty and find it easier to forgive those who come clean than those who deny or cover up their mistakes. And good riddance to the guy who dares to cheat on you! However, in most matters of the heart, your motto is, "To err is human."

56 POINTS OR MORE:

With a soul as generous as Mother Teresa's, you return good for evil, forget all injuries, and bury the hatchet quickly. In fact, when faced with injustice, you're more likely to feel sorrow than anger. But be careful: you're so tenderhearted and trusting, you run the risk of getting hurt, and can be blind when it comes to others' faults. On the other hand, a nature as forgiving as yours staves off the stress that can come from frustration and resentment. If you add a little caution to your compassion, you're likely to live a long and happy life.

18. What makes you a great team player?

Sooner or later, we're all asked to be part of a team. Discover the trait that makes you indispensable to any group. Nationally known motivational expert Dan Stockdale, author of *Six Tips for Taming the Tiger of Teamwork*, helps you identify your special assets.

1. **Who usually plans your family vacations?**

   a. You, pretty much on your own

   b. The whole family weighs in, votes, and helps out

   c. Everyone discusses it, but you make the final decision and arrangements

2. **Your idea of fun exercise is:**

   a. A walk around the mall

   b. Taking a class with a friend

   c. A backyard ball game with loved ones and neighbors

3. **What do you enjoy most about dinnertime?**

   a. Cooking a delicious meal everyone enjoys

   b. Conversations around the table

   c. Choosing the menu

4. **When you have a great idea but others resist it, you:**

   a. Offer another equally solid idea

   b. Go along with what the group thinks is best

   c. Figure out a different way to convince them

5. **If you have a plan to improve your work environment, you:**

   a. Go directly to the boss and suggest it

   b. Try to enlist a few colleagues to join you before presenting it

   c. Start making small changes that will show how great it could be

6. **If your son needed help setting up his new iPod, you'd:**

   a. Fiddle with it until you figured out how it worked

   b. Ask him to show you what he already knows about it

   c. Read the directions aloud and lend a hand when he got stuck

7. **If you switched on the blender and nothing happened, you'd:**

   a. Experiment with it to see what the trouble was

   b. Read the warranty to see if you could send it back for repair

   c. Blend your food by hand instead and worry about the machine later

Your Score

MOSTLY A'S:

You're the IDEA PERSON.

A creative visionary, your ingenuity inspires everyone around you and makes you fast on your feet, able to shift gears and come up with new solutions in a flash. "Your flexibility and lively mind are catalysts for the rest of the group, sparking their imaginations and keeping the dynamic lively and fun," says Stockdale.

MOSTLY B'S:

You're the TEAM'S DIPLO-MAT.

Every team needs one: that person who can negotiate and find a compromise even when viewpoints seem far apart. That's definitely you. "Through listening and putting yourself in everyone else's shoes, you know how to pull a team together and reach a consensus about the group's goals," says Stockdale.

MOSTLY C'S:

You're the TEAM CAPTAIN.

There's no team without a leader, and most of the time, you're it. Full of fire, integrity, and charisma, you enjoy taking charge and have a knack for motivating others. "With a high-octane energy level, can-do attitude, and gift for verbal persuasion, you set a powerful example that the rest of the group is happy to follow," says Stockdale.

19. How do people see you?

Ever wonder whether others see you the way you see yourself? "Studies show that there may be a big difference between what we think we project and how others really see us," says Lois B. Morris, author of *The New Personality Self Portrait: Why You Think, Work, Love and Act the Way You Do*. Discover the signals you're sending out so you can master them.

1. **You wear lipstick or gloss:**

   a. When you're going out

   b. Almost every day

   c. Hardly ever

2. **Running out on a quick errand, you'd probably wear:**

   a. A nice top and pants

   b. Khakis or jeans and a T-shirt

   c. Sweats

3. **Your friends say your conversational style is:**

   a. Quiet but attentive

   b. Chatty

   c. Balanced with lots of back-and-forth

4. **When you meet someone, your first gesture is usually to:**

a. Smile

b. Say hello and maybe add a few words about yourself

c. Shake hands

5. **If cornered by the most talkative person at a party, you'd most likely:**

a. Grin and bear it

b. Try to get a few words in where possible

c. Make an excuse and walk away

6. **You usually sit:**

a. Curled up in the most comfortable position possible

b. With your back straight and both feet on the floor

c. With your legs crossed

7. **If there were a break in conversation during a job interview, you'd most likely:**

a. Wait it out

b. Volunteer information about your accomplishments

c. Ask the interviewer a question

Your Score

MOSTLY A'S:

Your signals say you're A GIVER.

Generosity and an open heart—that's what others see in you. The tuned-in way you listen and the soft voice you use to respond signal the world that you're compassionate. Your posture, too, reveals that you're a caring soul. You are never bashful about reaching out to touch a person's arm when appropriate.

MOSTLY B'S:

Your signals say you're WITTY.

Start a conversation and the first thing everyone notices about you are all those bright, charming, humorous responses you give. Since your wit comes naturally, it makes others feel instantly lighter. Combined with your great sense of humor and your robust and easy laugh, it's no wonder you're such a sought-after friend.

MOSTLY C'S:

Your signals say you're ENERGETIC.

You have so much pep that you have a hard time sitting still. You speak with animated gestures, fidget if you're stuck in one place for too long, and are always eager to go the extra mile! "This kind of energy tells others that you're open to adventure, ready to act on a moment's notice, and capable of outlasting just about anyone," says Morris.

20. What makes you a "hostess with the mostest"? The secret's in your favorite china pattern.

"We found that the china pattern people are drawn to indicates their personal entertaining style," says Andrea McDonald, one of the country's leading china experts and owner of www.dishmatchers.com. "That's because there's a direct link between the dinnerware they prefer and the type of parties they enjoy hosting." So take a look in your china cabinet and discover what's really on your plate!

CLASSIC BLUE AND WHITE:
You're positively stress proof.

"Women drawn to blue-and-white china—which lends a serenity and classic polish to a room—never sweat the small stuff because they keep life simple," says McDonald. Your take-it-as-it-comes approach creates a home atmosphere as relaxing as a country retreat.

SIMPLE, ELEGANT BAND OR BORDER:
Your sophistication shines through.

"Please" and "thank you" are never far from your lips because manners and poise are extremely important to you. "If you love these elegant, fancy dishes, you also enjoy hostessing formal dinner parties where attention to detail and dressing to the nines is part of the fun!" says McDonald. You understand that elegance is not about expense but about planning, and you make every party a memorable event.

BRIGHT, BOLD, OR MODERN:
You're a fun-loving welcomer.

Can't resist the bright colors and eye-catching patterns of bold china? "You're a festive party-giver who has an easy, welcoming style," says McDonald. Your carefree, no-muss, no-fuss attitude makes your house everyone's favorite place to party.

A HOLIDAY PATTERN:
You're an all-American traditionalist.

If you love serving holiday dinners on china adorned with symbols of the season, you have a deep love of family and rituals. "You believe every day has the potential to be a celebration and you carry that spirit all year round," says McDonald.

FLORALS OR FRUIT:

You're warm and romantic.

According to McDonald, this delicate china pattern is preferred by the ultra-feminine hostess who adds a tender, personal touch to every party—from hand-decorated place settings to the guests' favorite foods. But it's your natural warmth and attentive listening skills that make your friends and loved ones feel special every time!

Lucy Ricardo set her I Love Lucy table with Franciscan's Ivy pattern.

21. What do people think of you? The answer is right on your lips!

There may be a powerful connection between your favorite lipstick shade and the way you communicate with others. "Color sends a strong signal about how we see ourselves and how we want to be seen," says Leatrice Eisemen, author of *Colors for Your Every Mood*. See what your lipstick is saying about you!

IF YOUR LIPSTICK IS BRIGHT RED:

Your communication style is HIGH ENERGY!

"Women who love this shade are energetic and driven," says Eiseman. It's no surprise that:

- You make sure you know a little something about everything and everyone.

- You leap into love and life with fiery enthusiasm; red causes a hormonal surge that makes you passionate!

IF YOUR LIPSTICK IS ORANGE:

Your communication style is HAPPY-GO-LUCKY CHATTERBOX.

To the ancient Chinese, orange symbolized joy, so it's no wonder "orange lipstick wearers are fun-loving social butterflies," says Eiseman.

- Your perfect evening is spent catching up with family and friends.

- Research shows folks who love to communicate are also great multi-taskers.

IF YOUR LIPSTICK IS DARK RED OR BROWN:

Your communication style is FRIENDLY CONVERSATION-ALIST.

These are the colors of the earth, and "women who choose them project that same dependability and nurturing influence," says Eiseman. It means that…

- You rate high on scales of honesty. You express yourself simply, using down-to-earth language.

- You bring a welcoming touch to your décor, creating a cozy nest that's perfect for intimate conversation.

IF YOUR LIPSTICK IS CLEAR GLOSS:

Your communication style is TELL-IT-LIKE-IT-IS TALKER.

Gloss-wearers are no-nonsense types who like to keep it simple, "which means speaking your mind without embellishing the facts," says Eiseman.

- Your balanced view makes it easy for you to stay neutral in sticky situations.

- Your wardrobe is full of classic staples. Direct types like you keep conversations short and sweet—getting right to the heart of the matter.

IF YOUR LIPSTICK IS PINK:

Your communication style is SOFT-SPOKEN.

"Women who like pink tend to be soft-spoken types who make their point gently," says Eiseman.

- Your soft touch puts people at ease. You're a natural stress-buster, since your relaxed manner is contagious.

37 percent of men say they like bare lips best—but when it comes to color, ruby red and hot pink top their list!

22. How loyal are you?

When it comes to loyalty, are you a true-blue trooper or as fickle as they come? Take this test to discover your faithfulness quotient.

Part One

1. **If your mate acts like a bozo while you're trying to impress your new colleagues, you:**

    a. Pretend he's not your partner. If you turn the other way, no one will suspect you're together.

    b. Pass out with embarrassment. How could he do this to you?

    c. Pat him tenderly on the back. You know insecurity makes him act silly from time to time.

2. **Your political party is running a real oaf for office in the next election. You:**

    a. Cast your vote for him anyway

    b. Write in your own choice

    c. Vote for the other guy

3. **You met most of your friends in:**

    a. High school

    b. The course of your adult life

    c. Grade school

4. **Your favorite soap opera heroine turns from virgin to vixen in one episode. You feel she's:**

    a. No longer worthy of your attention

    b. Been given a crummy script

    c. Got a terrific chance to change her character

5. **An acquaintance bad-mouths your best friend. Your first reaction is:**

    a. Confusion! Why say that in front of me? Should I tell my friend? Could it be true?

    b. Indignation! How dare she gossip about my buddy?

    c. Anger! What a tattling toad!

6. **You think marriage vows should be kept:**

    a. 'Til death do you part

    b. 'Til a spouse turns sour

    c. 'Til all the help in the world can't heal the hurt

7. **How long have you been going to the same hairstylist?**

    a. About a month. I change all the time.

    b. Ten years. I'm devoted.

    c. A year. I'll stick to my stylist until her scissors slip.

8. **If you knew that a family member had cheated the government on his taxes you would:**

    a. Try to get him to make amends

    b. Snitch. No matter how painful, he has to learn the difference between right and wrong.

    c. Help cover his tracks. After all, blood is thicker than water.

Part Two

1. **Lovers come and go but friends are for a lifetime.**

   Agree _____ Disagree _____

2. **I generally frequent the same little shops.**

   Agree _____ Disagree _____

3. **My country right or wrong.**

   Agree _____ Disagree _____

4. **My children may sometimes be a bit unruly, but I love them dearly all the same.**

   Agree _____ Disagree _____

5. **As long as I'm needed and appreciated, I wouldn't think of changing jobs.**

   Agree _____ Disagree _____

Your Score

For Part One, give yourself the following number of points for each answer.

1. a-3, b-5, c-7	5. a-3, b-5, c-7
2. a-7, b-5, c-3	6. a-7, b-3, c-5
3. a-5, b-3, c-7	7. a-3, b-7, c-5
4. a-3, b-7, c-5	8. a-5, b-3, c-7

For Part Two, give yourself 3 points for each statement with which you agree.
Add the scores from Parts One and Two.

39 POINTS OR LESS:
You're a pro at burning bridges.

When a romance or friendship shows signs of wear, you end it without second thoughts. You pride yourself on being a free spirit. You're also quick to judge others. If you're unwilling to vow loyalty to anyone but yourself, you may feel lonely. Why not try to cultivate lasting friendships? You just may find that when you give others your vote of confidence, they return it tenfold.

40 TO 55 POINTS:
You live by the rule, "Blood is thicker than water."

When it comes to family, no ties of loyalty could be stronger. Through thick and thin, you're there. However, when it comes to those who are not your relations, you're much less likely to offer your hand in unconditional friendship. In fact, you're fickle. Your closest acquaintances are those you have just made. And when it comes to romance, the road is often rocky and the relationship short lived. Learn to truly trust people outside your family. You'd be surprised at how sincere someone other than your own siblings can be.

56 POINTS OR MORE:
Faithful, steadfast, and true blue, you're the queen of loyalty.

Whether it's family, friends, co-workers, or political figures, you take an oath of loyalty and stick to it. No wonder you're so popular. Others sense your devotion and want to be your friend. Of course, you're the first person in whom they confide. Their secrets are always safe with you and they recognize and appreciate it. Although fidelity is a wonderful attribute, be careful you don't become too docile. When you feel someone has done you wrong, stick up for yourself. Speaking your mind or voicing an opposing view doesn't mean you're betraying a friendship.

23. What captures your heart?

1. **You'd love to spend a romantic week-end with your mate at:**

    a. A secluded cabin in the woods

    b. A luxurious seaside resort

2. **Your collection of sentimental souvenirs could fill a:**

    a. Trunk

    b. Scrapbook

3. **You'd rather your husband introduced you as:**

    a. My lovely wife

    b. The love of my life

4. **At weddings you get more choked up when the bride and groom:**

    a. Exchange vows

    b. Share their first dance as husband and wife

5. **If your husband gave you a great, big hug and smooch in public, you'd feel:**

    a. Slightly embarrassed

    b. Very special

6. **You'd love to celebrate a milestone anniversary by:**

    a. Having a lovely candlelit dinner at a favorite restaurant

    b. Being the guests of honor at a surprise party

7. **Which message would you prefer to display on a needlepoint pillow:**

    a. Good things come in small packages.

    b. Live life to the fullest.

8. **You'd prefer to receive a card from your man signed:**

    a. "Love and kisses"

    b. "Always and forever"

9. **Do you believe there's any truth to the old saying, "Too much of a good thing can be bad"?**

    a. Yes.

    b. No.

10. **If you were renewing your vows, you would like:**

    a. A simple ceremony with only your loved ones present

    b. A lavish affair with all your friends and family

Forty percent of couples say that honesty is the real "magic" ingredient in a long, happy marriage.

Your Score

NOTE: If your score falls equally between the two categories, read both descriptions since you share characteristics of both types.

MOSTLY A'S:

You are captivated by little things.

Sentimental and sensitive, you enjoy the simple pleasures of life: a bird in flight, sunrise and sunset, sweet nothings whispered in your ear. You cherish peace and quiet and would much rather share intimate moments with your partner at home than go to a big party—especially if it meant being the center of attention.

MOSTLY B'S:

Big displays of affection are what move you.

You have a taste for extravagance and a flair for drama, which explains why you adore grand-scale romantic gestures such as flowery love notes, big kisses in public, and noisy parties in your honor. Warm and bubbly, you're a pleasure to have as a friend and a joy to have as a marriage partner.

24. Do you need a pat on the back?

1. **At a potluck supper, your casserole is getting rave reviews. You:**

   a. Step forward and say, "Thanks"

   b. Smile but remain anonymous

2. **While flipping through your photo albums you notice most of the pictures:**

   a. Include you

   b. Were taken by you

3. **When you're having a tough time making a decision, you're more likely to:**

   a. Consult family and friends for their input

   b. Weigh the pros and cons by yourself. You don't want to bother anyone with your problems.

4. **When meeting new people you generally:**

   a. Talk

   b. Listen

5. **After an unusually demanding day you're more likely to:**

   a. Let off steam by venting to your husband or a close friend

   b. Put it behind you and delve into a project or chores

6. **If your birthday falls on a workday, you:**

   a. Drop a big hint!

   b. Keep it to yourself

7. **Which would you rather be?**

   a. A contestant on *Deal or No Deal*

   b. In the front row of Oprah's audience

8. **You're the Employee of the Week, with a plaque to prove it. You:**

   a. Display it

   b. Tuck it away with other special keepsakes

9. **Which would you prefer?**

   a. Public displays of affection

   b. Private words of appreciation

10. **You've just served your guests a complicated meal it took hours to make. As you sit down to join them, you focus on:**

    a. What went right

    b. What could be better

11. **When you splurge on a new outfit, it's because:**

    a. You deserve it

    b. You need it for a special occasion

Your Score

NOTE: If your score falls equally between the two categories, read both descriptions since you share characteristics of both types.

MOSTLY A'S:
You're a SHINING STAR.

Lucky lady! You intuitively understand that to be good to others you need to be good to yourself. So you accept praise as graciously as you give it, letting it go straight to your heart but not your head. That's why everyone feels your easygoing goodwill—and returns it twofold!

MOSTLY B'S:
You're an UNSUNG HEROINE.

Modest and humble by nature, you turn the spotlight on others—but you deserve some attention, too. Trust yourself! Basking in a well-deserved compliment or two won't spoil your modesty or make folks think any less of you. In fact, the glow you'll show will make you even more of a pleasure to be around.

Studies show that the majority of us would rather give compliments than receive them.

25. What makes you a great mate?

1. **You can tell from your midafternoon chat that he's having a bad day at work. You:**

   a. Prepare his favorite dish and let him vent

   b. Order take-out, rent his favorite movie, and help him unwind

2. **You tell your hubby you love him:**

   a. All the time

   b. Whenever the spirit moves you or you feel he needs a boost

3. **While walking in the park, you're more likely to be:**

   a. Strolling side-by-side, deep in conversation

   b. Walking hand-in-hand in comfortable silence

4. **When celebrating his birthday, you usually:**

   a. Ask him what his heart desires

   b. Surprise him

5. **After a disagreement, who usually apologizes first?**

   a. He does.

   b. You do.

6. **Lately, he's been getting a little self-conscious about his physique. You:**

   a. Lift his spirits by telling him he looks better than ever to you

   b. Tell him you love him the way he is but encourage him to join a gym

7. **When turning in for the night, you usually:**

   a. Snuggle for a bit

   b. Kiss each other and roll over to your respective sides

8. **How often do you and your mate get together with friends, without each other?**

   a. Once in a while

   b. Fairly often

9. **When it comes to making household decisions, you:**

   a. Basically agree with each other

   b. Often have to compromise

10. **Which weekend getaway would you prefer?**

    a. Anywhere you can be together

    b. Anywhere you can enjoy time apart and together

Your Score

Note: If your score falls equally between the two categories, read both descriptions since you share characteristics of both types.

MOSTLY A'S:
You light up his life.

You truly adore your husband and lavish him with attention every chance you get. Whether he's sharing his hard day at work or his dreams, you make whatever he has to say seem important. He thrives in the loving bond you've created through your intimate conversations and passionate connection. You cherish every moment spent with him, so it's no wonder he always feels on top of the world!

MOSTLY B'S:
You understand his needs.

Whether you're watching TV, making dinner, or running errands together, he's always charmed by your easygoing and nurturing attention. Skilled at reading his emotions, you know when he's in need of a hug and when to leave him be, a quality he treasures. You make him feel comforted and appreciated when he's in need of it most.

Seventy-five percent of wives and eighty percent of husbands say they consider their spouse their best friend.

26. Who is your best friend?

She encourages and supports you, listens and offers gentle advice—and she always seems to know just what to say when you need her most. The person you've chosen as your best friend says a lot about you. Why? "Your closest friend is like your twin soul. She reflects your core values and mirrors the most essential parts of your personality," says Patricia Gottlieb Shapiro, author of *Heart to Heart: Deepening Women's Friendships in Midlife*. If your best friend is:

YOUR SISTER OR MOTHER:
You're decidedly grown-up.

"Your relationship with your family is a complicated one, tinged with boundless love, old rivalries, heartfelt memories, and hot-button issues. If you're able to blend all those conflicting things into a wonderful friendship, then you've perfected an extremely sensible and adult view of life," says Shapiro. Your tastes run toward practical pumps rather than Mary Janes, soft neutrals rather than youthful brights—and happy-forever families rather than fleeting relationships. You'll always be there for your loved ones, and you want them to know it.

A FRIEND FROM WORK:
You reach for the stars.

"If you feel close to someone who knows what it's like to work where you work, then you're a big-thinking overachiever who's powered by a strong will to make a better life for your family," says Shapiro. You've got your priorities in order, and you strive toward elevating yourself and fulfilling your family's hopes and dreams whenever you can. Your philosophy is, "You'll never get anywhere if you don't try!" That's why you and your family are on the way up. Full-speed ahead!

YOUR HUSBAND:
You're down-to-earth.

"A woman whose closest friend is her husband tends to be a calm, down-to-earth doer who relates well to men because she shares a similar view of the world," says Shapiro. You take a practical, no-nonsense approach to almost everything. But practicality is no fun all the time, so, once in a while, surprise your best friend by slipping into a slinky, curve-enhancing gown. Just watch his eyes light up!

A PARALLEL-LIVES PAL:
You're comfortably content.

A parallel-lives friend is someone who's at the same stage in life that you are: maybe you've both got young children, you're both buying your first home, or you're recently retired. "If that's who you choose, odds are you're exceedingly comfortable and content with your life. Otherwise, you wouldn't seek out a best pal who is on the same path as you."

A GRADE-SCHOOL CHUM:
You're rock steady.

"Best friends from childhood have been together for years, through thick and thin—and if you see no need to change that, you've got a steady strength of character that's rare in today's fast-moving world," says Shapiro. You know that dependability beats novelty, whether it's your dish detergent or your family values. This smart attitude has helped you succeed for years—and you wouldn't change it for the world.

27. What makes you a perfect party guest?

Getting invited to a party is terrific, especially around the holidays. But did you ever wonder what gets your name on the invitation list in the first place? Maggie Gallant, a top-notch Hollywood party planner, has the answer! Take this quiz to find out!

1. **Which fun gathering is typically your favorite?**

   a. A big, all-out bash

   b. A hands-on potluck

   c. An intimate dinner party

2. **If you were wearing high heels and the dance music started playing, you would:**

   a. Kick off your shoes and dance, dance, dance

   b. Help the hostess pass the hors d'oeuvres

   c. Strike up a conversation with a shy wall-flower

3. **Your special party clothes are usually:**

   a. Daring—designed to make a statement

   b. Casually pretty and always comfortable

   c. Fashionable but rarely flashy

4. **For a kid's birthday party, you'd volunteer to:**

   a. Be the clown

   b. Bake the cupcakes

   c. Meet and greet the parents

5. **If you got a bad haircut, you would:**

   a. Wear a hat or playful barrettes until it grew out

   b. Fix it yourself

   c. Return to the salon and ask for help

6. **The makeup item most important to your party look is:**

   a. Lipstick

   b. Mascara

   c. Eye shadow

7. **As a housewarming gift for a new neighbor, you'd give:**

   a. A cute, personalized welcome mat

   b. Your special homemade dessert

   c. A bright flowering plant

Your Score

You love the limelight.

When there's a room full of people, odds are you're in the center of it all, keeping the other guests laughing with your quick wit, knack for storytelling, and humorous take on life. "You know how to work the room, enjoy the limelight, and aren't afraid to risk being silly if that's what it takes to make the evening fun," says Gallant. You're the one hosts count on to turn a downbeat party around.

MOSTLY B'S:
You're helpful and giving.

It's second nature for you to pitch in. "You were probably raised in a family where the best gatherings involved everyone," says Gallant. You also see helping out as a way to thank your hostess for her efforts. Odds are, it also makes the party more fun for you, too, since helping others and volunteering boosts levels of the brain's feel-good endorphins.

MOSTLY C'S:
You're a mingler.

No matter what kind of day you've had, when you get to a party, you enjoy chatting with everyone. Not usually shy, you're terrific at making introductions. "You make everyone feel important because you listen closely to what they say and are genuinely interested," says Gallant.

28. How well do you understand men?

He's tall, dark, and handsome—and next to impossible to figure out. If you find the opposite sex a bit of a mystery, take this revealing quiz.

Part One

1. **At the close of your first date, he kisses you and whispers, "I'll call soon." Expect your phone to ring:**

   a. The next morning, around the same time your alarm goes off

   b. Within the next couple of days; he's bound to call for a date

   c. Sometime before you collect Social Security

2. **Of these comments, which would most likely give a guy heart palpitations?**

   a. I want you to make a commitment.

   b. Your money or your life.

   c. Would you lend me your car?

3. **You tell a man you just want to be friends. In his mind, this means:**

   a. You'll have a casual relationship that may include sex.

b. You're just not in the mood for lovemaking at this particular moment.

c. You are interested in sharing good times— but that's it.

4. **The house is a mess, so you ask your partner to please help clean up before your company arrives. Which of these chores will he choose to do?**

a. Cleaning the kitchen and bathroom

b. Vacuuming

c. Keeping the pet hair off the couch by covering it with his body

5. **You tell your mate you're feeling blue. He suggests:**

a. Taking you to a ball game to cheer you up

b. Sharing feelings and getting to the root of the problem

c. You're being melodramatic

6. **Which of these films would a guy most want to see a sequel to?**

a. *Top Gun*

b. *Ten*

c. *Gone with the Wind*

7. **If a guy tells you he's not interested in marriage, although you are, you assume:**

a. You can always change his mind with time.

b. You'll hold on for a while, then look around for a more eligible bachelor.

c. He's not interested.

8. **As a special gift for your beau, you'd probably present him with:**

a. A silky negligee for yourself

b. Dinner at a nice restaurant

c. Two tickets to the theater

Part Two

1. **Men have a tough time showing their true feelings.**

Agree _____ Disagree _____

2. **If your man doesn't like your hairstyle, he's not likely to tell you.**

Agree _____ Disagree _____

3. **The only sure way to a man's heart is through his ego.**

Agree _____ Disagree _____

4. **Although men may act macho, they often like to be pampered like babies.**

Agree _____ Disagree _____

5. **Give most men some time in the kitchen and they'll make...a mess.**

Agree _____ Disagree _____

Your Score

For Part One, give yourself the following number of points for each answer.

1. a-3, b-5, c-7	5. a-5, b-3, c-7
2. a-7, b-3, c-5	6. a-7, b-5, c-3
3. a-5, b-7, c-3	7. a-3, b-5, c-7
4. a-3, b-5, c-7	8. a-7, b-5, c-3

For Part Two, give yourself 3 points for each statement with which you agree.
Add the scores from Parts One and Two.

39 POINTS OR LESS:

To you, men are a mystery. When you're involved with one you lose your usually reliable bearings and get lost at sea. Ironically, one reason you head in the wrong direction could be fear of failure. After all, fear closes down channels of communication. Instead of turning a deaf ear to problems, try to listen to what your man is saying. Many men have difficulty expressing their emotions, so get in the habit of encouraging your mate to talk about his feelings. Soon, you'll understand much more.

40 TO 55 POINTS:

You know the meaning of the phrase, "Boys will be boys." Generally, you have a good grasp of the opposite sex. You're rarely fooled by flighty men and have a keen sense of what makes the male ego tick. You might have grown up with older brothers who showed you the ropes. Now that you're an adult, you have opportunities to put your wisdom to work. Occasionally, however, you meet a man you think you can change. Remember, the only person you can change is yourself. When it comes to men, what you feel with your sixth sense is usually what you get.

56 POINTS OR MORE:

Perceptive and compassionate, you have a deep understanding of human nature. Your sensitivity helps you to focus on the similarities between the sexes, rather than the differences. As a result, men find it easy to share their feelings with you. Of course, there are occasional barriers. When this occurs, you intuitively tear down resistance by offering an attentive ear. You also know how to heal the male ego if it has been bruised by an unhappy past relationship. With you as diplomat, a truce could be declared in any war between the sexes!

29. What quality most impresses people about you?

Zero in on your most captivating quality and you'll win people over to your way of thinking. Travis Bradberry, PhD, author of *The Emotional Intelligence Quick Book*, says you can find the most impressive thing about yourself—and then learn to use it to your ultimate advantage.

1. **Of these, the character trait you think is your strongest is:**

   a. Friendliness

   b. Trustworthiness

   c. Decisiveness

2. **You'd describe your handshake as:**

   a. Somewhat firm

   b. Soft and warm

   c. Strong

3. **You're most likely to begin a call with a friend by saying something like:**

   a. I was just thinking about you.

   b. What have you been up to?

   c. I can't wait to tell you…

4. **You are interviewing for a job. Which of these behaviors will make the most memorable impression?**

   a. Making frequent eye contact and smiling when speaking

   b. Asking insightful questions, including one personal question about the interviewer

   c. Making a follow-up phone call or sending a thank-you note

5. **If the person behind you at the movies starts talking a lot, you:**

   a. Ask her to be quiet in a pleasant voice

   b. Turn around to give her a look

   c. Face the screen but whisper, "Shhhh!'

6. **Your toddler won't share and grabs his toy from another child's hands. You:**

   a. Tell him he needs to share and have him give the toy back

   b. Ask him if there's another toy he'd like to share

   c. Return the toy to the other child yourself

7. **If a co-worker took credit for your ideas, you'd:**

   a. Take her aside and privately suggest she correct her error

   b. Let it go—this time

   c. Politely correct her on the spot, in front of whoever was listening.

Your Score

MOSTLY A'S:

Your most impressive quality is your incomparable social skills.

No matter the situation or the person you're dealing with, you intuitively know what to say or do. That's because you recognize that others want to feel important and all it takes is some positive feedback. People appreciate this and "your outgoing nature rallies people to you," says Bradberry.

MOSTLY B'S:

Your most impressive quality is your ability to read others.

From the shift in their body language to the tone of their voice, you have no trouble reading other people. Your ability to put yourself in others' shoes drives this trait. And you're a good listener. "When you listen to what's on a person's mind, barriers are broken—and they'll be receptive to what you say," says Bradberry.

MOSTLY C'S:

Your most impressive quality is your independence.

When you enter a room, your confidence comes through in your posture and the way you walk. "When you have confidence, people feel sure about you and want to follow your lead," says Bradberry. Your self-esteem and take-charge qualities mean you're capable of setting forth a plan, but you also know how to compromise when it's necessary.

30. Do you follow your heart?

Part One

Mark the statement that you most agree with.

1.

a. Love makes the world go 'round.

b. Money makes the world go 'round, but love makes the ride worthwhile.

2.

a. I can read a person's true nature in an instant.

b. It takes time to really know someone.

3.

a. I'm an avid collector of mementos and souvenirs.

b. I clean out my closets regularly and avoid collecting knickknacks.

4.

a. I believe in fate.

b. I believe we control our own destinies.

5.

a. You can change someone through the power of love.

b. Only we can change ourselves.

Part Two

Complete the following:

6. To win the PTA's support for a project that's close to your heart, you'll:

a. Appeal to their humanitarian impulses with an impassioned speech

b. Organize and circulate a petition to support your cause

7. The supermarket's gourmet section is promoting some mouth-watering (but rather expensive) goodies. You're more likely to:

a. Treat yourself to the most tempting item

b. Make do with a few samples

8. In your dream biopic, which of these hunks would you cast as your leading man?

a. George Clooney

b. Tom Hanks

9. Your man could make your heart sing the loudest by:

a. Offering you a perfect red rose with a graceful flourish

b. Fixing all the leaky faucets in the house—without making you ask even once

Your Score

Note: If your score falls equally between the two categories, read both descriptions since you share characteristics of both types.

MOSTLY A'S:

Your heart rules.

A real romantic, you're in love with love. You laugh and cry easily and your reactions are genuine. This kind of sensitivity is admirable—but it can be overwhelming. Give your mind the reins sometimes…but never toughen up. Your charm lies in the fact that your heart is an open book.

MOSTLY B'S:

You stay balanced.

Passionate about being sensible, you listen to your heart but never let it dictate your actions. That's fine, but if your grounded approach starts weighing you down, try trusting your emotions and see how much sense your feelings make.

More than 51 million Americans (93 percent of them women) read at least one romance novel a year and spend over 1.5 billion dollars on the steamy books.

31. What's your mate really like? His favorite ice-cream flavor holds the key!

Can you get the real scoop on your mate's personality just by checking out his favorite ice-cream flavor? Yes! "Psychological studies reveal a direct link between ice-cream preference and personality type," says neurologist Alan Hirsch, MD, director of Chicago's Smell and Taste Treatment and Research Foundation. "Because our flavor choices develop around the same time as our personalities, they're firmly connected and deeply entrenched." So go ahead: try this cool way to find out what makes your man so sweet.

STRAWBERRY:
He's rock steady.

"Studies show that men who choose strawberry are logical people who make careful decisions," says Dr. Hirsch. That's not to say your mate is boring: just a steady provider who keeps your family on track. Your teenager's testy? The washing machine floods? Relatives show up for a surprise visit? Calmly, your husband offers quiet support and hands-on help. Preferring old-fashioned values to flights of fancy, he considers a loving family, a comfortable home, and a secure future life's greatest accomplishments. Lucky you! You have a husband who's also your guardian angel.

VANILLA:
He's an outgoing achiever.

Think vanilla-lovers are boring? Think again! "Our studies show men who favor vanilla tend to be gregarious and willing to help others," says Dr. Hirsch. And no wonder: research shows that the scent of vanilla acts on the brain to boost not only mood but generosity as well. Your guy never says no to a pal's request for help with his yard, a chance to hang out with his friends, or the opportunity to put in overtime so he can advance at his job. And although he's content with his hectic schedule, he always makes time to get a smooch from you at the end of the day.

COFFEE:
He's the life of the party.

"Coffee ice-cream lovers are lively and energetic—they're real life-of-the-party types," confirms Dr. Hirsch. At parties, your husband plays the perfect host or regales others with jokes, and he's no different at home: upbeat and positive, he whistles a cheerful tune even while mowing the lawn! For your hubby, life's a bowl of cherries—with coffee ice cream on top!

CHOCOLATE:

He's a born romantic.

Scientists say love at first sight and the taste of chocolate both release a similar mood-boosting brain chemical. So it's no surprise that chocolate fans are romantics who know how to put their family first. Playfully passionate, your partner holds your hand in public and tells your friends you're gorgeous. If the kids need a boost on the softball field or with their chores, his can-do enthusiasm gets them going.

BUTTER-PECAN:

He's an ace problem-solver.

Bring it on: "A detail-oriented guy who sets high standards for himself and others, your husband loves a challenge," says Dr. Hirsh. If something needs fixing, from the roof to the family budget, your guy takes charge and gets the job done. Why? The butter-pecan personality sees tasks like these as a chance to prove himself to everyone, and he gets satisfaction from winning. So score big with him by letting him know he'll always be a champion in your book.

32. Are you addicted to love?

Do you often confuse lust with love? This quiz might help you learn to distinguish between the sizzle and the steak—and turn that red-hot beginning into a long-lasting relationship.

Part One

1. **Basically, you're attracted to a certain kind of guy. He's:**

   a. A hunk—tall, dark, and handsome; real swoon material

   b. A lamb—sweet, sensitive, and sensual; not gorgeous but always gracious

   c. A cad—romantic and riveting; he plays the field and is a high scorer

2. **Speaking of men (aren't we always?), let's say you meet one who lets you know he's not interested in getting serious. You think:**

   a. Maybe that's what he thinks now, but I know I can change him.

   b. I'll stick with him for a while, but, if the situation remains stagnant, I'm splitting.

   c. So long. I'm not interested in a frivolous affair.

3. **As a teenager you loved to read:**

a. Adventure stories

b. Sappy romances

c. Celebrity biographies

4. **When you read the newspaper you turn first to the:**

a. Lifestyle section

b. International, national, and local news pages

c. Celebrity gossip

5. **On average how long do your romances last?**

a. More than five years

b. More than six months

c. Five weeks, tops

6. **Your very best friend introduces you to her new boyfriend and (horrors!) you instantly feel uncontrollably attracted to him. What do you do?**

a. Flirt

b. Fantasize

c. Forget it

7. **You feel most comfortable wearing:**

a. Lace and velvet

b. Silk and satin

c. Pure cotton and cashmere

8. **Which of these statements best describes your feelings about love?**

a. It needs to be cultivated if you want it to last.

b. If you keep your heart open, it's always available.

c. It's a wonderful once-in-a-lifetime experience.

Part Two

1. **I stay interested in a man even if he's not available.**

Agree _____ Disagree _____

2. **When I see couples kissing in public, I'm inspired.**

Agree _____ Disagree _____

3. **Nothing makes me feel more glamorous than falling in love.**

Agree _____ Disagree _____

4. **The world would be a better place if we were ruled by our heart, not our head.**

Agree _____ Disagree _____

5. **I know practically all the lyrics to the latest love songs.**

Agree _____ Disagree _____

Your Score

For Part One, give yourself the following number of points for each answer.

1. a-5, b-3, c-7	5. a-3, b-5, c-7
2. a-7, b-5, c-3	6. a-7, b-5, c-3
3. a-3, b-7, c-5	7. a-5, b-7, c-3
4. a-7, b-3, c-5	8. a-5, b-7, c-3

For Part Two, give yourself 3 points for each statement with which you agree.
Add the scores from Parts One and Two.

39 POINTS OR LESS:
You are sensible and down-to-earth.

You know the difference between love and a lighthearted fling, but, rather than searching for romance, you let it find you—and when it does, you embrace it with open arms and an open heart. Not one to fool yourself, you never pretend you can change a man. You know better! That's probably why you're likely to fall in love for life. It's not the thrill of romance that makes you feel alive, but the cozy comfort of a calm relationship. The lucky man who chooses you as his partner will share the warm, simple values of family life.

40 TO 55 POINTS:
You are optimistic and trusting.

You try hard to distinguish between innocent flirtation and real-life romance, but, unfortunately, you sometimes confuse love with lust. Perhaps that's why you fall for more lines than Little Red Riding Hood. Some men really are the big, bad wolf, although you might pretend otherwise. ('Fess up: you sometimes enjoy being fooled!) Although you really believe you're looking for the love of a lifetime, a part of you still wants romance more than a gold ring. You're not ready to settle down right now—so enjoy yourself.

56 POINTS OR MORE:
You are addicted to love.

No two ways about it, you would rather fall in love than be in love. You're addicted to the thrill of the new and still mysterious romance. Once a relationship starts to grow, you get bored and begin the hunt all over again. In actuality, commitment and security are scaring you away. But you must have romance in your life or risk feeling empty, worthless, and at odds. It may be a hard thing to change, but it's probably low self-esteem that keeps you addicted to love. You need to build inner confidence. Start today by making a list of your strengths and keep it growing. Before long you'll start a new chapter in your life.

33. In whom do you confide?

Something great happens—or something awful happens. You've got a great idea—or a huge secret. Who's the person you tell? The answer reveals a hidden truth about your personality. "When it comes to a woman's closest confidantes we almost always choose the person who best mirrors and enables our natural tendencies and life view," says Susan Newman, PhD.

IF YOU CONFIDE IN YOUR HUSBAND:
You're a down-to-earth doer.

"Women whose closest confidant is their husband tend to be calm, grounded types who relate well to men because they share a similar view of the world," says Newman. Never one to give in to wild displays of emotion, you take a practical, no-nonsense approach to life. Women who name their spouse as their closest confidant are most often the ones who stay married for life.

IF YOU CONFIDE IN YOUR MOTHER OR SISTER:
You're a rock-steady traditionalist.

They were the first and most solid relationship you had. "Women who still confide in their mother or sister have a deep need for stability, continuity, and history," says Newman. You draw your strength from your family and your past, always preferring traditional values over the latest pop culture.

IF YOU CONFIDE IN YOUR DAUGHTER:
You're open-minded and flexible.

Generation gap? Not on your life! "Women who are close to their daughters tend to score high on scales of flexibility and open mindedness," says Newman. This deep friendship with someone so much younger not only reflects on your forward-thinking modern attitude, but also your ability to change with the times.

IF YOU CONFIDE IN YOUR BEST FRIEND:
You're naturally stress-proof.

Women who have a very close friendship with another woman and confide in her frequently experience less stress than others. Why? They instinctively know how to calm themselves almost before they get agitated. Even better, research shows women who report close friendships rate highest on happiness scales and tend to live longer.

The number-one attribute women look for in a husband is a good sense of humor—but in a friend, it's honesty.

34. Can you read him like a book?

1. **You offer your husband advice and he looks down. He's probably:**

   a. Uneasy about admitting he needs you

   b. Thinking your advice over

2. **When a man wears a pinkie ring, you can be sure he:**

   a. Pays attention to his appearance

   b. Is creative

3. **You asked your man to pick up milk, but he forgot. When he didn't offer an apology, you figured it was because:**

   a. He couldn't admit that he was wrong.

   b. He felt guilty.

4. **After your first evening out together, your date nonchalantly utters, "I'll call." You:**

   a. Wait a week and see

   b. Expect a call in the next day or so

5. **While you're talking to your mate, he leans on his elbow, chin propped in one hand. This means he's:**

   a. Lost in his own thoughts

   b. Hanging on your every word

6. **If your man says he doesn't want to talk about his feelings, it means he:**

   a. Prefers to work things out for himself

   b. Has something to hide

7. **Your guy's signature slants to the right, meaning he's an:**

   a. Extrovert—emotional and charming

   b. Introvert—reserved and sensitive

8. **If a man you've been dating for a month gives you a self-timing coffeemaker for your birthday, it's because he's:**

   a. Considerate; he wants to make your life easier

   b. Not attracted to you in a romantic way

9. **He rubs his nose while explaining why he's late, letting you know that he:**

   a. Could be stretching the truth

   b. Might be coming down with a cold

10. **When a new boyfriend asks you about your before-he-came-along relationships, it's usually because he:**

    a. Wants to know everything about you

    b. Is feeling insecure

Researchers say that 80 percent of what we "say" is communicated through gestures rather than words.

Your Score

Give yourself 3 points for each "a" answer and 1 point for each "b."

IF YOU SCORED 26 TO 30 POINTS:
Your vision is 20/20.

Open minded and receptive, you can read your partner like a book, responding intuitively to his every glance and gesture. It's your ability to clearly see him and your life together—the wonders as well as the occasional trouble spots—that has made your relationship so strong. Sharing such an easy rapport, it's no surprise why you and your mate are best friends.

IF YOU SCORED 20 TO 25 POINTS:
Glasses recommended.

Most of the time, you get the message, but an occasional signal or two sneaks past your radar. And although your mate knows without a doubt how much you love him, why let a few crossed wires come between you and clear communication? Even if you're almost sure you know what he's getting at, ask directly—and make a clear connection!

IF YOU SCORED 14 TO 19 POINTS:
Glasses required.

It's not that you can't read his signals... you've just been misinterpreting them. But even though you often miss the precise meaning of his hints, it's easier than you might think to "refocus." Simply put yourself in his shoes when evaluating his next puzzling word or action. With a little effort, you'll be reconnected in the blink of an eye.

35. Are you a great friend? The answer is in your favorite ice-cream topping!

I scream, you scream, we all scream for ice cream—but did you know that the topping you scream for reveals a secret about you: what kind of friend you are! "Whether you prefer to indulge in something soft and gooey or sweet and chewy, there's a powerful connection between how you treat yourself and how you treat those closest to you," says Eileen Mastrio, director of marketing for Friendly's ice-cream shops. So pick your favorite topping and get the real scoop on why you're so popular.

CANDY:
You're a kid at heart.

If you crave candy toppings, odds are you've never completely traded in your knee socks for

a pair of pantyhose. "You approach friendship with the same youthful, childlike spirit that enhances most other parts of your life, and that keeps matters lighthearted and fun," says

Mastrio. Quick to make new friends, you're easygoing and a joy to be around. And just like the candy topping you love, you're as sweet as can be.

SPRINKLES OR JIMMIES:
You're an inspiration!

Checking off a to-do list? Meeting unreasonable deadlines? Sticking to a strict diet? Not you! "Just like the wacky, colorful toppings they crave, spontaneous sprinkle-lovers long for adventure rather than routine!" says Mastrio. You don't need to scale Mount Everest, but you do love taking calculated risks that make your life that much more interesting. Whether you're redecorating your home in a bright summer color or taking a spur-of–the-moment weekend trip, your special brand of confidence inspires friends to dive right in and make a splash—and nothing, not even sprinkles, can top that.

CHOCOLATE OR HOT FUDGE:
You're cheerful and confident.

Lots of people crave chocolate because it contains a feel-good chemical called phenyl ethylamine that works by stimulating the brain's pleasure center and gives us a warm happy glow. "That's why you love it, too—because it gives an extra boost to your naturally sunny personality," says Mastrio. Never one to feel down in the dumps for long, you can always find a reason to smile. Upbeat and content, you know that friends are worth their weight in gold, so you treat them like priceless treasures.

FRUIT TOPPING, SUCH AS STRAWBERRIES OR PINEAPPLE:
You're definitely diplomatic.

For you, life is a bowl of cherries—because you know how to avoid the pits! "Those who prefer the grown-up pleasures of fruit rather than sugary candy or chocolate tend to be tactful and diplomatic, even in the stickiest situations," says Mastrio. Whether you're refereeing your kids' argument or defusing a problem at work, you're a model of smooth sophistication. No fumbling or mumbling for you; you're always able to come up with the perfect friction-free, fluster-free responses!

BUTTERSCOTCH:
You're the life of the party.

There's nothing subtle about luscious, creamy butterscotch topping. "If this distinctive flavor is your choice, you've got a charismatic, flamboyant approach to life that means no one around you is ever bored!" says Mastrio. Pals flock to you, attracted by your spunky get-up-and-go attitude and the excitement they feel when they're around you.

NUTS:
You're loyal.

Walnuts, pecans, crushed peanuts…these toppings have been on ice-cream parlor menus for generations. "If you choose good, old-fashioned nuts, you're a loyal person who has kept the same friends since your school days," says Mastrio. Why? Because you know that tried-and-true almost always beats slick-and-new, especially when it comes to pals! Your friends know they can always count on you, too—and your true-blue friendship enriches the lives of everyone lucky enough to win it.

Part Three

Your Career

1. Discover your goal-reaching strategy.

"Each of us has an innate approach to solving problems that we may not even be aware of," says Stephen Shapiro, author of *Goal-Free Living*. This quiz will help you uncover the traits that guarantee your success.

1. **When you encounter an obstacle, you:**

   a. Weigh whether you're chasing the right goal

   b. Decide it's best to change your approach

   c. Stay on course and work harder to solve the problem

2. **If you were working on a group project, you'd volunteer to:**

   a. Come up with a creative presentation

   b. Pitch in on a variety of tasks as needed

   c. Handle the research

3. **If you wanted to change your hairstyle, you'd:**

   a. Trust your stylist to suggest something

   b. Ask for something dramatic and go for it

   c. Collect pictures and discuss them with your stylist in detail

4. **If you were single and wanted to be in a relationship, you'd**

   a. Go places where men might be likely to congregate—clubs, classes, etc.

   b. Ask your friends to set you up

   c. Look for the best professional or online dating services

5. **When you make a mistake, your first reaction is:**

   a. "Oh well, I'll do better next time."

   b. "How do I keep this from snowballing into a bigger problem?"

   c. "Where did I go wrong? I don't want to make this mistake again."

6. **You would describe your current job as your:**

   a. Destiny: what you were meant to do.

   b. Passion: what you love to do.

   c. Livelihood: what you need to do.

7. **When it comes to scheduling, you:**

   a. Write things down, but stay open to changes

   b. Rely on your memory instead of the calendar

   c. Stick closely to your date book

Your Score

MOSTLY A'S:

Your strategy is your POSITIVE ATTITUDE.

Other folks may feel overwhelmed when there's too much on their plate, but not you! You keep going strong and never let anything dampen your upbeat spirit. That's because you see life's challenges as opportunities. "It's your ability to stay positive in the face of any obstacle that guarantees you'll meet your goal," says Shapiro.

MOSTLY B'S:

Your strategy is that you LIVE IN THE PRESENT.

Some people are always making plans for tomorrow and missing what's right in front of them. But not you! Whether you're dealing with a crisis or spending time with loved ones, you always experience the moment. And because of your present orientation, you pick up on important details around you—a trait that will help you advance further and faster, according to Shapiro.

MOSTLY C'S,

Your strategy is that you STAY FOCUSED.

Once you make up your mind, nothing can shake you. That's because whether you're handling a crisis, mapping out your future, or planning a family outing, you rely on your rock-solid focus and sharp organizational skills. "You have the ability to keep your eyes on the prize, stick to your goals, make solid plans, and stay on schedule," says Shapiro.

2. What really motivates you?

Part One

You...

1. **Are doing the kind of work you've always wanted to do:**

    a. True

    b. False

2. **Prefer to go clothes shopping by your-self—you don't want a second opinion!**

    a. True

    b. False

3. **Serve a meal knowing it's delicious because you've given it your personal taste test.**

    a. True

    b. False

4. **Raise your children according to your own philosophy, rarely asking for advice from others.**

    a. True

    b. False

5. **Have a home-decorating style that really says, "YOU!"**

    a. True

    b. False

6. **Have always known what you wanted to be "when you grow up."**

   a. True

   b. False

7. **Have been wearing the same fragrance for years and have no desire to change.**

   a. True

   b. False

8. **Go to your hairstylist with a description of the exact cut you want.**

   a. True

   b. False

9. **Have always known exactly what qualities you are looking for in "Mr. Right."**

   a. True

   b. False

Part Two

10. **Your local cable station has asked you to host a weekly show. For the first installment, you:**

    a. Do what you do best—talk about topics that are close to your heart

    b. Decide on a topic and invite a variety of local experts to discuss it

11. **To encourage your daughter to try out for the track team, you:**

    a. Talk to her about the importance of having a dream and going after it

    b. Show up at the trials to cheer her on

Your Score

Note: If your answers are closely divided between the two categories, read both descriptions, since you share characteristics of both types.

MOSTLY A'S:

You have inner drive.

You have always known in your heart and soul what you want to achieve in your life. Whether it's raising a family, working at a job, decorating your home, or choosing a wardrobe, you never look to others to show you the way. Your self-confidence and powerful inner drive help motivate you to fulfill your dreams.

MOSTLY B'S:

You have outer rewards.

You relish taking on a challenge, and, whether it's a new project at the office or a fundraiser, your work is always top notch and earns the appreciation of others. Their compliments inspire you to set your sights even higher. You're open to the opinions of others and are flexible in your approach to life. You seek advice before forming an opinion or taking action. This openness to outside possibilities motivates you to achieve excellence.

About half of us would sneak a peek at the diary of a family member or close friend to see if we're mentioned!

3. How do you overcome work hassles? There's a clue in your favorite movie classic.

Nothing's more satisfying then settling in to watch a movie you've loved for years. "Studies show we're drawn to particular film classics not merely for entertainment, but because we identify strongly with the way a character overcomes obstacles," says New York City psychoanalyst Gail Saltz, MD. So pick your favorite flick and discover how you deal with real-life drama!

GONE WITH THE WIND:
You're ingenious.

Strong willed and resourceful, there's nothing Miss Scarlett sets her mind to that she can't do. And if her tale of love and war ranks as your favorite, you're the same way. "Feisty and full of ideas, you always figure out how to hold down the fort," says Dr. Saltz. When there's work to be done, you roll up your sleeves and see the job through with a steadfast focus. Plus, your bright ideas make you an all-important ally for co-workers who count on you to come through in a pinch.

STAR WARS:
You're courageous.

"If *Star Wars* is your favorite, you probably admire the courage of its characters, especially Princess Leia, whose fighting spirit and willingness to take a chance helps save the day," says Dr. Saltz. When risks need to be taken and quick decisions made, you leap into the fray, acting on instinct and trusting your gut to tell you what to do. And guess what? Most of the time, you're right on target! Whether it's hiring a new employee on the spot just because you have a good feeling about her, or firing off a memo to protest a new work policy, you're not afraid to rely on your own decisions—and that's made you the success you are.

CASABLANCA:
You're levelheaded.

In *Casablanca*, Ingrid Bergman's character, Ilsa, sacrifices love so others may be free. "Like you, she weighs the consequences before arriving at the best course of action," explains Dr. Saltz. This levelheadedness means you stay calm in the face of chaos. When your boss assigns you a report that's due the next day, you don't panic. You pause, take a few deep breaths, and figure out the best way to turn the situation to your advantage.

THE SOUND OF MUSIC:
You're optimistic.

The hills are alive not only with the sound of music; they're shining with your upbeat, optimistic outlook! "Just like Maria von Trapp, you dream of a better world, and you encourage those around you to keep on hoping and striving," says Dr. Saltz. When office morale is low, you're the one who can spark esprit de corps and get the team back on top. You have a sixth sense that tells you when colleagues need emotional and hands-on support and you offer it willingly because you know that a positive attitude can get everyone through even the toughest times.

THE GODFATHER:
You put family first.

Sure, you like your job—but, just like the members of the Godfather clan, there's never been any question in your mind: family comes first. "No matter what else is going on in your life or on the job, you keep your mind focused first on the welfare of your family," says Dr. Saltz. Whether it's lending a hand in your child's classroom or whipping up homemade snacks for Sunday afternoon football, you do it with pleasure. Your heart positively bursts with love and family pride, and your husband and kids know there's nothing you wouldn't do for them—even if it means putting your career success on hold.

4. Discover your leadership potential.

1. **It's time for the annual neighborhood potluck supper. You'll be:**

   a. Phoning everyone to remind them about it

   b. Cooking up a storm

   c. Organizing everything, from the menu to the table arrangement

2. **You're worried that your husband's recent weight gain will affect his health. You:**

   a. Remind him how sexy, handsome, and irresistible you found him when you first met

   b. Join him on a diet-exercise program

   c. Cook him lots of low-calorie meals and stock the pantry with plenty of healthy snacks

3. **You have a great idea that will eliminate a lot of extra work at the office. You:**

   a. Post a memo for all, explaining your plan's benefits

b. Take steps to put your plan into action

c. Organize your plan step-by-step and call a meeting with co-workers to explain your ideas and get some feedback

4. **When your six-year-old wants to learn to ice skate, you:**

a. Walk out on the ice with her, offering your arm for support

b. Skate alongside her, showing her how to make some simple moves

c. Sign her up for lessons and take her to them each week

5. **When it comes to planning family vacations, you're the one who:**

a. Orders tons of travel brochures on destination you're considering

b. Takes over once the trip begins

c. Makes reservations, finds someone to watch the house and take care of the pets, and stops the mail delivery

6. **You and your best friend decide you both need a makeover. When you arrive at the salon, you:**

a. Insist she go first, then rave over the job they're doing on her

b. Sit right in the stylist's chair and tell her to give you a new look

c. Plan the day from hair cutting to clothes shopping to buying makeup

Your Score

MOSTLY A'S:

You're a cheerleader.

Your enthusiasm is the key to your leadership style. When you believe in something, there's no way to keep it a secret. Your boundless, positive energy is contagious and acts as a beacon to others. Your enthusiasm is usually appreciated, but be careful. Sometimes it can be overpowering.

MOSTLY B'S:

You're an example setter.

You're a woman who believes in personally setting an example. You know the best way to help someone learn something is by demonstrating it yourself. In fact, you never suggest anything unless you've already tried it. Whether it's a project at work, within the family, or for the community, you encourage others to join you by adopting a hands-on approach.

MOSTLY C'S:

You're a guiding light.

You're a genius in advocating, planning, and making things happen. Your well-developed organization skills complement your leadership style. Although you may not actually get involved in a hands-on way, you are a guiding force from the seed of an idea to the end result.

5. What gives you the winning edge?

We all have goals, but the "force driving us to achieve them is often hidden—even from ourselves!" says Rosaline Glickman, PhD, author of *Optimal Thinking*. Uncover yours with this quiz!

1. **Upon arriving home from the supermarket, you realize you've been overcharged by $5. You:**

   a. Seek a refund the next time you shop there

   b. Set the receipt aside, but probably forget about it

   c. Drive back right away

2. **If the book you're reading becomes boring in the middle, you probably:**

   a. Finish it anyway

   b. Skip to the good parts

   c. Move on to something you enjoy

3. **When the phone rings, you usually:**

   a. Let it ring a few times before picking up

   b. Let your answering machine get it

   c. Hurry to answer it right away

4. **If you won a lot of money, you'd spend it on:**

   a. An investment opportunity

   b. A dream home or car

   c. Making a fantasy come true—such as taking a dream vacation or buying a piece of fabulous jewelry

5. **If you were involved in a play, the job you'd most want is:**

   a. Director

   b. Stage manager

   c. Lead actor

6. **It's the third day of a new diet and someone offers you a fabulous dessert. You:**

   a. Politely decline

   b. Share it with a friend

   c. Enjoy a small slice

7. **If you reach a two-way stop sign at the same time as another driver, you:**

   a. Wait and let the other car go

   b. Make eye contact to size up who should move first

   c. Try to go first

Your Score

MOSTLY A'S:

Your winning edge comes from WILLPOWER.

Once you decide on a course of action, you stick with it and let nothing get in your way. That's because you see yourself as the master of your own destiny! "Willpower is fueled by the dominant personality traits of restraint, resolve, and discipline," says Glickman. You've got plenty of all three, so even when your energy lags, you don't stop until you get the job done.

MOSTLY B'S:

Your winning edge comes from FLEXIBILITY.

"If you hit a detour, you don't feel frustrated, you just try to figure out how to make the alternate route work for you!" says Glickman. Naturally open minded, you have a knack for considering all points of view before reaching a decision. This "big picture" approach helps you adapt to any new situation or overcome an unforeseen obstacle with ease.

MOSTLY C'S:

Your winning edge comes from PASSION.

No matter what you take on, you bring your whole heart and soul to it, making it your new "cause." For you, if there isn't a flame burning deep inside, there's no reason to get involved with a project. And your drive to leave your mark makes you positively unstoppable! Eager to try new things, your boundless spirit keeps you moving forward.

6. Discover your secret to success.

Each of us has an innate approach to how she gets what she wants in life. Stephen Shapiro, best-selling author of *Goal-Free Living* and founder of www.goalfree.com, offers this quiz to help you uncover your best approach to success!

1. **If you were considering switching careers, you would:**

   a. Visualize what you want and trust that success would find you

   b. Use your passion as a barometer and determine your best course of action

   c. Create concrete plans with detailed steps and execute each step in turn

2. **When you encounter an obstacle, you:**

   a. Stay on course and know you'll find your way eventually

   b. View it as an opportunity to change your approach

   c. Dig your heels in and work harder than ever to solve the problem

3. **In regard to your own happiness, you might say to yourself:**

   a. "I'm in charge of creating my own happiness."

   b. "I'm happy now and have just what I want."

   c. "I will be happier when _____ (fill in the blank)."

4. **If you were single and wanted to be in a relationship, you would:**

   a. Fantasize about the man you want to meet, knowing that eventually he'll appear

   b. Have a great time socializing rather than focusing on that perfect mate

   c. Research several options for finding a guy and then pursue the best ones

5. **If you were having a hard time getting your three-year-old to settle down for a nap, you'd:**

   a. Allow him to stay up, knowing he'll sleep when he's exhausted enough

   b. Put him to bed and stay quietly in the room until he settles down

   c. Tuck him in with his favorite teddy bear, kiss him, and let him know you'll be back when nap time is over

6. **When it comes to opting for a new hair-style, you:**

   a. Gaze in the mirror imagining how you'll look with the new cut

   b. Just go for it

   c. Discuss it carefully with your stylist before doing it

7. **When it comes to scheduling, you:**

   a. Write one down but stay open to changes

   b. Don't bother mapping one out. You just do whatever is pressing at the moment.

   c. Make time management a priority

8. **If there's a group project to be presented at work or in the community, you volunteer to:**

   a. Come up with a really creative way to present it

   b. Float from one task to another

   c. Volunteer to do the research. You love surfing the Web.

9. **If you make a mistake, your first reaction is to:**

   a. Believe that everything happens for a reason

   b. Appreciate the experience it's given you

   c. Commit to trying harder next time

10. **Your current job is your:**

    a. Destiny: what you're meant to do

    b. Passion: what you love to do

    c. Livelihood: what you need to do

Your Score

MOSTLY A'S:

You stay POSITIVE.

As a born optimist who sees the silver lining inside every cloud, you believe in destiny and trust that the universe has just the right plan for you. Seeing the big picture and visualizing what you want out of life truly works for you. And scientific studies confirm that this approach really scores results! To give your upbeat attitude even more power, Shapiro says, "Don't wait passively for success to find you. Be proactive, too." Make a list of what you want to accomplish in the short term, write down steps that will lead you there, and keep your goals manageable. With your upbeat attitude and a little grounding, you can make anything happen.

MOSTLY B'S:

You stay PRESENT.

As a woman who lives for today, you are largely motivated by the moment-to-moment process of working towards achieving your goals, not necessarily the end result. Rather than focusing on one project or goal, your tendency is to keep your options open and consider all possibilities. Shapiro puts you in the category of "goal-free" people. "Because experiences matter more than your accomplishments," he says, "your natural curiosity draws you in." Stay focused by working in a distraction-free environment and taking mini-breaks if your interest flags.

MOSTLY C'S:

You stay FOCUSED.

Your strategy for success: set your goals in stone, make solid plans, and stick to a tight timetable. Rather than looking at the big picture, you're more comfortable taking it one step at a time, relying on facts rather than imagination or instinct, and analyzing all your decisions carefully. This cautious approach means your focus stays strong. To give your success strategy a boost, Shapiro suggests taking a few more chances. "Stay open to possibilities and explore other avenues by asking 'what if' questions and reminding yourself that even if you do make a mistake, you can learn from it!"

7. Uncover your destiny!

Ever wonder what you were meant to do? "Let your core talents guide you to a life that's satisfying," says career consultant Patti Fralix of www.fralixgroup.com, author of *How to Survive in Spite of Mess, Stress and Less.* Take this quiz to discover your true calling.

1. **You spend your extra money on:**

   a. Books or magazines

   b. Crafts or hobbies

   c. Fun impulse purchases for everyone

2. **Which of these blank books would you be most likely to fill?**

   a. Address book

   b. Photo album

   c. Journal

3. **Which of the following is most true?**

   a. You're a thinker whose mind is always working.

   b. You're a creator who enjoys making things.

   c. You're a collaborator who does her best work in groups.

4. **Your ideal work environment would be:**

   a. A quiet office

   b. Fast-paced and always changing—maybe with some travel

   c. Someplace close to home with flexible hours

5. **Planning an afternoon with the kids? You'd probably choose to:**

   a. Visit a museum

   b. Take a walk in the park or spend time in the playground

   c. Invite their friends to join you for ice cream or pizza

6. **You'd describe the way you dress as:**

   a. Classic or conservative

   b. Eclectic

   c. Casual or sporty

7. **Of these, you'd get the greatest sense of satisfaction from:**

   a. Devising a successful savings plan

   b. Finishing a home-decorating project

   c. Volunteering for a worthy cause

Your Score

MOSTLY A'S:

You're meant to put your problem-solving skills to work.

Curious and analytical, you love playing detective. If there's a puzzle to be solved, you'll know just what to do. "Your core talent is the ability to assess a situation, so people look to you for direction," says Fralix. That's why any kind of consulting job, from business manager to therapist, would suit you perfectly!

MOSTLY B'S:

You're meant to tap into your creativity.

With your inventiveness and your super-powered imagination, you have a true appreciation for beauty. "Tuned in to your senses, your core talent comes from a visual aesthetic with a hands-on approach," says Fralix. Choose a creative career such as landscaping, decorating, even selling handmade items.

MOSTLY C'S:

You're meant to channel your compassion.

Naturally empathetic, you can always sense what others need and you probably feel happiest when you've made a difference. "Driven by a sense of purpose and compassion, you're a real humanitarian," says Fralix. You are likely to find your destiny in the helping professions, working for nonprofit organizations or teaching.

8. Who's your career mentor?

Take this quiz to discover which money-making mentor you're most like. "Finding out could reveal your path to success," says Jim Canterucci, author of *Personal Brilliance.*

1. **You search for good deals on trendy clothes at:**

   a. Big discount stores

   b. Secondhand or thrift shops

   c. Boutique sales racks

2. **You'd be likely to leave an extra set of house keys:**

   a. With a neighbor or friend

   b. In a secret hiding place

   c. Inside your car's glove compartment

3. **If you could have the top-of-the-line of one of these, you'd choose a:**

   a. Designer outfit

   b. Electronic item, such as a flat-screen TV

   c. First-class ticket to somewhere spectacular

4. **When you have lots of spare change, you usually:**

   a. Try to spend it so you can hold on to your big bills

b. Stack it on your dresser and grab it as needed

c. Save it in a jar until it's full and then cash it in for bills

5. **The section of the newspaper you turn to first is:**

   a. Style (or society/celebrity)

   b. National news

   c. City or local section

6. **Of these experts you'd be most interested in hearing:**

   a. Dr. Phil

   b. Anderson Cooper

   c. Suze Orman

7. **The game of chance you'd most enjoy playing is:**

   a. Bingo

   b. Lottery

   c. Slots or roulette

Your Score

MOSTLY A'S:

Your mentor is Oprah Winfrey.

Even if you had a million (or billion!) dollars, odds are you'd balance investing in the future with sharing the wealth—just like your alter ego, Oprah Winfrey. Compassionate, uplifting, and deeply spiritual, you'd be the kind of money-maker who gives great paying jobs to friends, embraces a charity or two—but never takes for granted the perks of the high life.

MOSTLY B'S:

Your mentor is Bill Gates.

What makes Bill Gates a success? His flair for finding unusual solutions to problems. Just like him, you often have several get-rich ideas percolating at once. "The secret to your success will be zeroing in on one idea and devoting the energy to see it through," says Canterucci.

MOSTLY C'S:

Your mentor is Donald Trump.

When it comes to money, you've got Trump's sensibilities: you're a bold risk-taker with a knack for spotting money-making opportunities. "Tapping into your Trump-like optimism will get you through any financial rough spots and clear a path for the brightest future possible," says Canterucci.

9. What success secret is hidden in your household clutter?

Hate clutter? You're not alone: 91 percent of American women say it's their biggest housekeeping hassle. But before you sweep it under the rug, listen to this: experts say the place your clutter accumulates most is an excellent indicator of your secret strengths! How so? "Clutter tends to build up most around the places we expend our greatest mental and physical energy," reveals Marilyn Paul, author of *It's Hard to Make a Difference When You Can't Find Your Keys*. Here's what your mess says about your success!

If your clutter's primary location is your . . .

FRONT HALLWAY:
Your secret key to success is relaxation.

"Clutter in the front hall means you subconsciously feel a strong separation between your public and private lives, and you're so eager for one not to encroach on the other that you literally 'drop it' at the door," says Paul. No matter how busy your career, you're a homebody at heart!

BEDROOM CLOSET:
Your secret key to success is polish and pizzazz.

"The jumble of dresses, blouses, shoes, purses, and scarves you collect isn't a sign of vanity, but rather success: you know that being perceived as polished is half the battle when it comes to getting ahead in life," says Paul. So go ahead and play dress-up. It's not just fun, but a worthy investment in your future.

DESK OR HOME OFFICE AREA:
Your secret key to success is control.

Receipts, old bills, letters . . . Do you keep every scrap of paper you might need to handle your home or finances? "Folks who do tend to be superior managers who are great in a crisis because they can stay in control," says Paul.

COFFEE TABLE:
Your secret key to success is knowledge.

What's the most common clutter on coffee tables? Newspapers, magazines, and books! "Folks with this kind of clutter tend to be information-seekers with an inquisitive mind and a deep curiosity about the world around them," says Paul.

KITCHEN TABLE:
Your secret key to success is friendship.

"The kitchen table is the heart and center of the house, a powerful symbol of sharing and caring," says Paul. "And the more cluttered yours is, the more your top priority is nurturing your family and bonding with friends."

What do American women say is the most cluttered area of their closet? The jumble of shoes on the floor!

10. What was your worst subject in school? Surprise! It reveals your talents today!

Remember your school days? There were classes you loved, but then there were those subjects that just couldn't hold your interest. Experts say there's a good reason for that! "We're drawn to subjects that are compatible with our strongest personality traits and our natural talents and skill—and we dislike those that are at odds with who we are inside," explains Jill Spiegel, co-founder of Goal Getters, a motivational and career consulting firm. Discover the hidden gifts that put you at the head of the class!

If you hated . . .
MATH:
You're passionate.

Turned off by math? "People who lack an interest in math find it too cool for their naturally passionate, intense nature," explains Spiegel. Not only do you give 100 percent of your heart and soul to everything you do, but you're likely to:

- Leap before you look—whether it's falling in love or trying a new hairdo.

- Surround yourself with shades of red, at home and in your fashion choices. Red is the color chromologists link to intensity and excitement.

ENGLISH:
You're a go-getter.

Read other people's stories? Not on your life! "Students who dislike English are action-oriented types who would rather live their own adventures," says Spiegel. So it's no surprise that:

- You're a fidgeter. Not only can't go-getters like you sit still, but toe-tapping helps you concentrate.
- You are probably more coordinated than the rest of us.

GYM:
You've got inner peace.

"Rather than someone whose adrenalin boost comes from competitive sports, this is a person who enjoys solitude and quiet reflection," says Spiegel. It means:

- You often contemplate the meaning of life and ask for guidance from a higher source.
- You take plenty of time before making decisions, weighing the pros and cons.

Believe it or not, chewing gum and playing music in the background might actually help boost concentration while studying.

SCIENCE:
You're a social butterfly.

Forget those long, lonely hours spent in the lab—that's just not for you. "Women who were turned off by studying science tend to be outgoing and sociable," says Spiegel. No wonder you:

- Have a wardrobe filled with attention-getting styles
- Express your feelings easily, which puts others at ease

HISTORY:
You're spontaneous.

"History is about making sense of the past, but people who say it's not for them prefer to live in the moment—or envision the future," says Spiegel. You also:

- Are just unpredictable enough to keep your partner interested and on his toes
- Learn from your mistakes and move on

FOREIGN LANGUAGES:
You're a creative whiz.

"Folks who find themselves bored with foreign languages tend to be creative types who are more likely to make up their own 'code' languages than conform to existing ones," says Spiegel. And you:

- Never follow the same routine for more than a day or two. To you, shaking things up makes even the most humdrum activities seem interesting.
- Are a huge movie fan. Creative types tend to be visually oriented.

11. How ambitious are you?

Part One

Would you ever . . .

1. Work overtime just to impress the boss?
   a. Yes
   b. No

2. Go cold turkey when starting a diet by getting rid of all the sweets in the house?
   a. Yes
   b. No

3. Organize a big family reunion with relatives from all over the country?
   a. Yes
   b. No

4. Suggest a way to improve your work environment?
   a. Yes
   b. No

5. Consider starting an after-school program for neighborhood kids?
   a. Yes
   b. No

6. Take a voluminous novel out of the library and finish it before it's due?
   a. Yes
   b. No

7. Crochet an elaborate afghan?
   a. Yes
   b. No

8. Ask for a promotion?
   a. Yes
   b. No

9. Work on a 10,000-piece jigsaw puzzle?
   a. Yes
   b. No

10. Take an adult education class that will help you advance on the job?
    a. Yes
    b. No

11. Accept new projects when your schedule is already full?
    a. Yes
    b. No

Part Two

12. The walls in your home could use some freshening. You:
    a. Decide to paint them
    b. Do a little touching up where it's most needed

13. Which of the following most closely describes the way you feel about your life?
    a. "I'm generally happy but I can think of a few changes I'd make to improve my situation."
    b. "I can't think of anything I'd change about my life."

14. Take a walk down Memory Lane. When you were in high school, you …
    a. Got involved in extracurricular activities: student council, drama club, team sports
    b. Spent your time hanging out with friends

Your Score

Note: If your score falls equally between the two categories, read both descriptions, since you share characteristics of both types.

MOSTLY A'S:
You're DRIVEN.

You have a natural urge to get ahead, accomplish big tasks, and take advantage of opportunities. This enterprising spirit drives you to greater heights, whether it's improving your household, excelling on the job, or undertaking community or crafts projects. What others might find overwhelming, you consider a challenge. This attitude feeds your driving ambition and leads you to success. Just make sure you try to balance your busy day with some simple, stress-free pleasures.

MOSTLY B'S:
You're SATISFIED.

You couldn't be happier with the way things are! You enjoy your home life and job and rarely feel the need for change. This kind of pure optimism and contentment is healthy. Since you don't feel a driving force to get ahead at work or fill your day with challenging projects, you have plenty of time for your family and friends. When opportunity knocks, you always weigh your priorities carefully before answering its call.

Did you know that 60 percent of women polled report that they're responsible for keeping track of the household finances, and more than half pay all bills?

12. Unlock the power of your secret element.

According to Laurie Beth Jones, author of *The Four Elements of Success*, everyone's personality is aligned with one natural element: earth, wind, water, or fire. Find yours and put its power to work for you.

1. **If you could watch one TV show tonight, you'd pick a:**
   a. Legal whodunit such as *Law and Order* or *CSI*
   b. Decorating or fashion show such as *Trading Spaces* or *What not to Wear*
   c. Gossip or reality show such as *Entertainment Tonight* or *America's Next Top Model*
   d. Sitcom such as *The Office*

2. **Of these, you're more likely to read a:**
   a. Newspaper
   b. How-to book
   c. Fashion or women's magazine
   d. Novel

3. **Which of these colors would you be most likely to try on your bedroom walls?**
   a. Rose or lilac
   b. Taupe, sage green, or gray
   c. Sky blue or aqua
   d. Cream or white

4. **Visiting your hairstylist? You'll most likely:**
   a. Choose a similar style to the one you have now
   b. Opt for something a little different that's easy to maintain
   c. Trust your hairdresser to do what'll look best on you
   d. Try something totally different

5. **The last time you shopped for a new purse, you:**
   a. Bought the first one that looked and felt right
   b. Took your time weighing several styles
   c. Consulted a girlfriend and went with her suggestion
   d. Couldn't decide and left with two

6. **When you invite friends over for dinner, you usually:**
   a. Plan and prepare a sit-down meal
   b. Set up a buffet of your specialties
   c. Have a potluck where everyone brings a dish
   d. Let your friends help prepare and serve the meal

7. **When it comes to organizing your day, you typically:**
   a. Make sure to complete one major task
   b. Methodically finish everything on your list
   c. Handle things on an as-needed basis
   d. Tackle many different projects at once

Your Score

MOSTLY A'S:
Your element is FIRE!

Confident and passionate, fire types have an impressive ability to meet obstacles head on. A natural fit for your driven personality and never-say-die attitude is running your own business, managing a team, or organizing a fund-raiser.

MOSTLY B'S:
Your element is EARTH!

"Reliable and stable with a solid sense of purpose, you're the type people know they can count on," says Jones. Generous and supportive like the earth, you're the consummate team player who is happiest offering guidance or helping everyone.

MOSTLY C'S:
Your element is WATER!

"Water is capable of changing form and water types are flexible and easygoing," says Jones. A born diplomat, your skills are best used where you can serve as a mediator—helping people on opposite sides come together.

MOSTLY D'S:
Your element is WIND!

"Just like the wind, you give 'breath' to ideas," says Jones. Your creativity often sweeps everyone along. Since your imaginative spirit gets restless with routine, you do best in creative fields such as design, where every day feels different.

13. Could you be a billionaire?

"Billionaires are all highly independent, creative, ambitious, and natural leaders," says career coach Stacy Mayo. Find out if you have what it takes and get quick tips to increase your odds of becoming a billionaire!

1. **If you came into an inheritance, you'd:**
   a. Put half into a risky but promising start-up business
   b. Invest after speaking to a financial adviser
   c. Put it in the bank

2. **To resolve a disagreement, you typically:**
   a. Try to convince people to see it your way
   b. Come to a compromise
   c. Let the other person win

3. **If your gas station raised its prices 10 percent, you'd:**
   a. Check around for a better deal elsewhere
   b. Continue to go there because it's convenient
   c. Walk or ride a bicycle more often

4. **Do you worry about what other people think of you?**
   a. Not much
   b. From time to time
   c. More often than you'd like to admit

5. **What would stop you from asking for a promotion?**

   a. The new position might not be as interesting as your current job.

   b. You might lack some of the necessary skills.

   c. You have a fear of rejection.

6. **You mostly read:**

   a. Biographies

   b. Self-help

   c. Fiction

7. **You're considering renovating your bedroom. You:**

   a. Trust your own sense of style

   b. Balance your instincts with a few tips from others

   c. Listen carefully to friends' advice

8. **Which most closely describes the state of your wallet at this moment?**

   a. It's orderly and you know exactly what's in it.

   b. It's messy but you have an idea about the amount in it.

   c. It's disorganized and you don't know what you have.

9. **If you hit the jackpot your first time at a slot machine, you would be likely to:**

   a. Take your winnings and try a new game

   b. Play for a while, but stop when your winnings drop too much

   c. Pocket the money and walk away

10. **How comfortable would you feel going to the movies or dinner alone?**

    a. Very uncomfortable

    b. You could manage

    c. No problem—You enjoy your own company

Your Score

MOSTLY A'S:

You've got what it takes to be a billionaire!

Your natural tendencies to dream big, take charge, and get ahead lead you to the kinds of risks and opportunities that are destined to pay off—if they haven't already! "Your ability to turn problems into possibilities is the number one characteristic of all billionaire personalities," says Mayo. But all this ambition also means you push yourself pretty hard physically, emotionally, and mentally. To reduce stress and restore balance to your life, try:

- Just sitting still. Enjoying five minutes of quiet in a comfortable chair every day can recharge your body and mind by releasing endorphins and lowering blood pressure. Repeat a simple word such as *one* or *peace* to clear you mind, and concentrate on your breathing rather than your to-do list.

- Getting a goldfish. Studies show that watching fish swim has a calming effect.

MOSTLY B'S:

You've got billionaire potential.

Your confidence and self-assurance mean you could easily steer you own path to riches. But you do such a good job balancing home and work that often you're too happy with everything to risk messing it up. To step out of your comfort zone and hit the jackpot:

- Talk to a buddy. Reluctant risk-takers are more likely to take the plunge if they get support from others.

- Give yourself a reward. People who treat themselves to something nice once in a while are more likely to seek out the challenges that will lead to promotions and a bigger paycheck.

Success is yours—if you want it!

When it comes to taking the lead in ways that could pay off big, you often second-guess yourself and let your lack of confidence keep you from stepping forward. "To make it big, you have to believe in your natural power and talents," says Mayo. She suggests writing down all you've accomplished in your life, because putting achievements in writing can make confidence double. Next:

- Design a strategy to get ahead by setting an attainable goal each day, even if it's as simple as organizing your desk.

- Do what billionaires do when they have a setback: ask yourself what you can learn from it.

14. Which celebrity entrepreneur do you most resemble?

They're known for TV and movies, but many celebrities also strike it big in business. "Just like them, you have an entrepreneurial trait that can make you rich," says Walter P. Pidgeon Jr., PhD, author of *CEO Workbook*. Take this test to identify yours!

1. **Do you consider yourself a risk taker?**

   a. Not really

   b. Sometimes

   c. Absolutely

2. **How do you feel when meeting new people?**

   a. You're a little uncomfortable at first.

   b. You enjoy it.

   c. You're at ease enough to learn from the interaction.

3. **You'd prefer a job that:**

   a. Lets you work from home

   b. Includes opportunities to travel

   c. Is a short drive from home

4. **You take a leadership position:**

   a. Only when necessary

   b. Often

   c. Almost always

5. **You'd describe your main career objective as:**

   a. Providing extra income for your family's needs

   b. Doing something you enjoy and can be recognized for

   c. Making a difference in the world

6. **Other than your computer, the item on your desk you glance at most is:**

   a. A framed picture of your family or pet

   b. Your daily appointment book

   c. A to-do list

7. **If you had a choice, the color scheme you'd use for your work area would be:**

a. Earth tones

b. Brilliant primaries

c. Pastels

Your Score

MOSTLY A'S:

Your celebrity match is KATHY IRELAND.

Former supermodel Kathy also has a home-furnishings empire. With a similar love of home, you'll come up with a money-maker by making life better for busy moms. Pidgeon's suggestion: "Think: products that simplify chores!"

MOSTLY B'S:

Your celebrity match is JENNIFER LOPEZ.

Glamorous J Lo launched a sexy clothing line and perfume business. Like her, you've got an eye for beauty. So, focus your entrepreneurial energies on products or services that help women look great, and you'll thrive.

MOSTLY C'S:

Your celebrity match is OPRAH WINFREY.

With a strong moral compass, Oprah has no trouble rallying others to change the world. Like her, you like to make a difference. Pidgeon's advice: Link causes with making a living—whether it's kids, animals, or the environment.

15. Find your personal get-organized strategy!

We'd all love to be more organized, and the key lies in recognizing the personality traits that can help us—or stand in our way! Sara Pedersen, founder of www.time2organize.net, helps you unlock the personality secrets that can keep you clutter free.

1. **When it comes to a junk drawer, you:**

a. Don't have one

b. Use it rarely for odds and ends

c. Have one so stuffed you can barely open it

2. **Your everyday purse is:**

a. Tiny—just big enough for a lipstick, wallet, keys, and a cell phone

b. Medium-size

c. Oversize

3. **Of these, which would you be most likely to buy at a yard sale?**

a. Something electronic

b. An article of clothing or jewelry

c. An antique pitcher or other collectible

4. **When it's time to find your keys, you:**

a. Know right where they are

b. Check one or two main spots

c. Often have to hunt for them

5. **To remember birthdays and anniversaries you:**
   a. Mark them in your diary or calendar
   b. Need someone to remind you
   c. Memorize the dates

6. **If a friend peeked in your closet, she'd discover:**
   a. An organized and useful wardrobe space
   b. A place jam-packed with clothes, accessories, and shoes
   c. Lots of clothes she's never seen, since you keep the clothes you wear most often in piles or on chairs

7. **When doing your grocery shopping, you:**
   a. Always take a list
   b. Often just buy what you need for a day or two
   c. Walk up and down the aisles, picking up what seems right

Your Score

MOSTLY A'S:
You're on top of everything.

You always know what's going on in the news, at your job, and in your family. It's this tendency to stay totally connected that can help you eliminate clutter. How? "Since you're always up-to-date, you don't need to keep yesterday's papers or the magazine clippings you're saving for 'someday,'" says Pedersen. Tossing all that extra paper will help make your kind of clutter vanish.

MOSTLY B'S:
You're easily inspired.

A creative whirlwind who lives in the moment, you throw yourself into each new project that intrigues you, but then set it aside when something else piques your interest. The result: lots of unfinished business piling up around you. Pedersen suggests using your gusto to get organized. How? By tackling only one cluttered space at a time and never spending more than thirty minutes on it—ensuring that your enthusiasm won't lag.

MOSTLY C'S:
You're reflective.

A sentimental soul, you have a hard time letting go of souvenirs that remind you of special times. Pedersen says your connection to the past can work in your favor, actually helping you get organized. How? Use your nostalgic impulses as a reminder that it's the memories that matter most—not the stuff associated with them. Then, find a more practical and compact way to preserve your souvenirs, such as a scrapbook or memory box.

16. Could you work from home?

"Working from home takes extra self-discipline, organizational skills, and the ability to ignore distractions such as the television, phone, and refrigerator," says Priscilla Y. Huff, author of *101 Home-Based Businesses for Women*. Find out if you've got what it takes.

1. **Which do you enjoy most?**
   a. Working on a project alone
   b. Leading a team
   c. Lending a hand

2. **As a general rule you follow a:**
   a. Weekly plan
   b. Daily plan
   c. No plan—you deal with tasks as they arise

3. **To get the facts fast you usually communicate:**
   a. By e-mail
   b. By phone
   c. Face-to-face

4. **Feedback from co-workers and higher-ups:**
   a. Is not something you need
   b. Is sometimes helpful; a simple "good job!" can spur you on
   c. Is essential in helping you evaluate your work

5. **Most of your closest friends are:**
   a. Folks from outside your job
   b. Co-workers past and present
   c. A mix of co-workers and others

6. **Your work space:**
   a. Has a place for everything and everything is in its place
   b. Looks disorganized but you know where to find stuff
   c. Is the symbol of a creative mind—a mess!

7. **If there's a monotonous task needing attention, you:**
   a. Do it right away to get it over with
   b. Finish something first and then get back to it
   c. Take a break to reenergize

8. **At work when people talk about a TV show you love, you:**
   a. Listen with one ear, but keep working
   b. Jump in with a quick comment and get right back to work
   c. Join the conversation

Your Score

MOSTLY A'S:

You're a natural work-at-homer!

You've got the motivation, discipline, and focus to join the 26 million Americans who work from home. "You find office chatter more distracting than the quiet of your home office," says Huff. But there are ways to recreate what you might be missing from an office situation. Here's what Huff suggests:

- Give yourself a break at least twice a day. Research shows just getting up from your desk to stretch your legs brings fresh blood to the brain, increasing your ability to think creatively.

- Create a network of other work-at-homers with whom you can meet regularly. You'll build a support system and enjoy a break from the isolation of constantly working alone.

- Don't let work spill from your home office into the living room, kitchen, or bedroom. It can create clutter that adds to your stress level.

- Have a definite end to your day. Studies show that home workers are more likely to burn out because they keep going well past the conventional eight-hour workday.

MOSTLY B'S:
You thrive on a balance of work and home.

Sure, you've got what it takes to work from home, but you also enjoy the connection you have with co-workers. For you, a mix of office time and home time is perfect. To make the most of every minute you're at home:

- Work in two-hour blocks. Workers are most productive for no more than two straight hours.

- Work according to your body clock. If you feel energized in the morning, really push yourself during those hours.

- Keep the boundaries clear. "Put up a *Do Not Disturb* sign on your office door so your family will know when not to bother you," says Huff.

MOSTLY C'S:
You're happiest when home and work are separate.

You function best with clear boundaries that keep your job and family separate. So here's how to accomplish more on the job and keep work from invading your private time.

- Don't multitask. When you stop a particular task and jump to another, your brain needs fifteen minutes to find its place when you go back to Task One. The result: You lose hours in your work week.

- Delegate. Letting go of less important items on your to-do list frees you, and shows you that easing up a little doesn't have as big an impact as you might think.

17. Are you in the right job?

Do you love your job? If not, maybe it's time to explore other careers. Take this test to see which occupations suit you best.

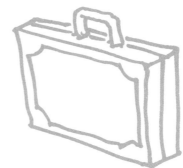

1. **You feel the most comfortable and confident when you're wearing:**
   a. Casual slacks or jeans, and sneakers
   b. Classic separates
   c. Expensive, elegant, up-to-the-minute fashions

2. **The PTA needs help fund-raising and asks those with special skills to volunteer. You agree to:**
   a. Be in charge of child care while parents are canvassing the neighborhood for donations
   b. Take on bookkeeping responsibilities
   c. Organize the entire project from scratch

3. **Faced with the challenge of having to speak in front of a large audience, you'd:**
   a. Turn down the opportunity. You don't like to be the center of attention.
   b. Muster up the courage
   c. Welcome the chance to entertain an audience

4. **If you had the opportunity to travel to an exotic country, you would:**
   a. Hike or bicycle, and camp out whenever possible
   b. Join a tour to have the company of fellow travelers
   c. Hire a personal guide

5. **A friend needs help moving. You suggest she:**
   a. Rely on you since you enjoy physical activity
   b. Enlist a bunch of friends to help; you'll make the calls
   c. Get an experienced moving company to do the work. You'll help her to find the best one.

6. **The handyman you hired didn't do the job quite right. How do you feel about telling him to redo it?**
   a. Uncomfortable. Frankly, you'd rather just do it yourself than ask him to fix it.
   b. Okay. You've learned to request changes in a pleasant, noncritical way.
   c. Fine. Giving orders is second nature to you.

7. **How important is it for you to stick to your daily schedule?**
   a. Not at all. You enjoy life's more spontaneous moments.
   b. Fairly important. You feel more comfortable when your day is somewhat structured.
   c. Very important. You follow your schedule to the letter and always structure every free moment.

Your Score

Give yourself 3 points for each "a" answer, 6 points for each "b," and 9 points for each "c."

21 TO 33 POINTS:
You're a FREE SPIRIT.

Based on your free-wheeling nature, you'd thrive in a job that incorporates your love of the outdoors, sense of adventure, and creativity. Consider taking a position in a children's day-care center or teaching young kids, and you'll always be creatively challenged.

34 TO 51 POINTS:
You're METHODICAL.

You enjoy a certain amount of routine, you're responsible, and you can handle many tasks at once. Employers appreciate your dedication and ability to get along with others. You'd excel as a manager or bank teller—or perhaps a mediator, because you're also skillful at smoothing ruffled feathers.

52 POINTS OR MORE:
You're HIGH-PROFILE.

The jobs that would make you happiest are those that put you in the limelight. You enjoy talking and dealing with people, and you consider a well-groomed appearance a must. Careers such as public relations, advertising, or politics would put you in the public eye and suit you to a T.

According to the to the U.S. Department of Labor, career areas set to experience the biggest boom include computer technology, health services, and social services.

18. Could you be the next "apprentice"?

Do you think you have the right stuff to be Donald Trump's next "apprentice"? "It takes a perfect mix of being fast on your feet and being a problem-solver, team player, and strong leader," says Carolyn Kepcher, a longtime high-level Trump employee and author of *Carolyn 101: Business Lessons from The Apprentice's Straight Shooter*.

1. **Your boss asks you to work with someone you know is difficult. You:**

    a. Have an upbeat meet-and-greet to rally support for your goals

    b. Lay down the law, spelling out your expectations

    c. Ask if you can work with someone else

2. **What's the best way to boost the morale of people who work for you?**

    a. Say thank-you for a job well done

    b. Express interest in their families and hobbies

    c. Have weekly coffee and doughnut get-togethers

3. **You're the boss and there's a crisis close to the end of the workday. What's your strategy?**

    a. Recruit top problem-solvers to find a solution

    b. Insist everyone stay late and pitch in

    c. Work through the night alone

4. **Which of these leadership styles is most effective?**

    a. Delegating

    b. Collaborating

    c. Being involved with everything

5. **You make a mistake at work. You:**

    a. Think about how to avoid making the same mistake again

    b. Apologize profusely

    c. Try to justify your error

6. **At work you believe it's most important to be:**

    a. Honest

    b. Kind

    c. Correct

7. **What color suit would you wear if called to the board room?**

    a. Black or gray

    b. Pastel or white

    c. Bright red or blue

Your Score

MOSTLY A'S:

You'd make a perfect apprentice!

Confident and inquisitive, "you're the type everyone sees as the indispensable go-to person," says Kepcher. More important, no matter what situation is presented, you command it with strength, integrity and character." No question, you're ready to step higher on the ladder to success. Here are some proven ways to do it:

172

- Reassess your goals every three to six months and kick them up a notch beyond what you know you can do. For example, if you feel ready to do work on a new project, reach for supervising it. People who reach higher really do achieve more!

- Find a mentor. Someone with more experience than you can serve as a trusted confidant and give you the inside track on how to move ahead, advises Kepcher.

- Don't skip lunch! Expand your network by asking co-workers to lunch. Colleagues are far more likely to share advice—and tips about job openings or promotions—during casual meetings.

MOSTLY B'S:
You'd give them a run for their money.

With your ability to delegate as well as your innate kindness and eye for quality, you'd make it to *The Apprentice* finals. "These traits are essential for every successful employee," says Kepcher. "But to make the leap to successful entrepreneur, you'll need to temper your inclination to be overtly modest." To accentuate your intelligence and accomplishments:

- Volunteer for high-visibility assignments that really showcase your talents, such as planning the office picnic or organizing a charity project.

- Pat yourself on the back—literally. It works like a hug to boost confidence.

MOSTLY C'S:
You're a maverick.

You're fueled by creativity, a zest for challenges, and a flair for following your instincts. "This kind of strong individualism means you'll make a terrific entrepreneur in your own right," says Kepcher. But if you want to be on Trump's team, "you might need to focus more on collaborating." To be a top-notch "apprentice":

- Don't be afraid of mistakes. They almost always lead to solutions. Surveys show that employees who don't own up to their mistakes is the number one pet peeve of CEOs!

- Listen hard! Totally tuning in greatly reduces the chance of making mistakes.

Carolyn Kepcher, who was Donald Trump's sidekick on the first few seasons of his television show The Apprentice, was purposely made to look older. At the time of airing, she was only thirty-five years old.

19. Feng shui your work space

Is your desk cluttered, neat and orderly—or something in between? "How you arrange your work space reveals how you approach the world," says feng shui expert Jayme Barrett, author of *Feng Shui Your Life*. Take this quiz to discover what your work area says about you— and get tips on rearranging your space to suit your natural temperament.

1. **Your wastepaper basket is:**
   a. Big and overflowing
   b. Small and emptied frequently

2. **You keep your pens and pencils:**
   a. In several places
   b. In a special holder

3. **Your calendar or desk diary is:**
   a. Sometimes missing a date or two
   b. Always up-to-date

4. **Do you keep a telephone directory in your office?**
   a. No.
   b. Yes.

5. **Which of the following would you most like to add to your workspace?**
   a. A couch
   b. A bookshelf

6. **You prefer to work:**
   a. With music in the background
   b. In silence

7. **Do you keep more than one personal memento (such as a photograph or souvenir) on your desk?**
   a. Yes.
   b. No.

8. **When you doodle, you usually:**
   a. Scribble away
   b. Trace the same intricate patterns

9. **You would rather have your desk facing:**
   a. The window
   b. The door

10. **If you were heading up a new project at work, you'd choose as your assistant:**
    a. The person you get along with best
    b. Someone you know is the most efficient

Your Score

Give yourself 10 points for every "a" answer and 5 points for every "b."

90 THROUGH 100:
You're OPEN-MINDED.

You may not have a perfect place for everything, but you know where everything is—and that's what matters most. An original thinker, you're happiest when working in a free-wheeling, inspiration-charged atmosphere. "You enjoy expanding your mind and considering all the options before reaching a conclusion," says Barrett. This approach means you keep on going, but it also means you find routine dull, and sometimes lose interest in projects before they're done. Making the most of your high-intensity work style is easy with these feng shui tips:

- Bring in a big couch. The cozier your office, the more you'll feel at home working there, even if you're a little bored by the task at hand.

- Get a round rug. "Big-picture thinkers need their ideas grounded, and a round rug does just that," says Barrett.

- Keep a red envelope with several coins in it on your desk. According to the principles of feng shui, this promotes profit, something supercreative people often have a hard time focusing on.

75 THROUGH 85:
You're a TEAM PLAYER!

Your desk is as much a reflection of your personality as your work style: Alongside the projects you're working on are family photos and souvenirs, because you like to keep a balance between your personal life and work life. You're flexible and willing to compromise, so it's no wonder so many colleagues list you as their favorite co-worker. But as a naturally easygoing person, you may find it difficult to assert yourself. Try Barrett's feng shui power boosters:

- Turn your desk to face the door. It will give you a heads-up on who's coming, so you're prepared for anything.

- Use a high-backed chair. It projects power, so your ideas will be seen as more solid.

- Hang a picture of a lotus flower. It symbolizes great achievements from humble beginnings!

70 OR LESS:
You're an OVERACHIEVER!

Highly organized, you see streamlining your office and keeping everything in its proper place as a way of staying on top of details. "Your ability to prioritize and focus on set plans means you may be less able to alter a course of action without feeling stressed," says Barrett. To add a bit of calm to your workspace, Barrett suggests that you:

- Place a picture of a lake on your wall. It will remind you to relax and go with the flow at all times.

- Hang a crystal from your window. The movement of light brings energy in, helping you focus on all the possibilities that lie ahead.

- Keep a jade plant in your room. Plants with round-tipped leaves are believed to round out or relieve stress.

20. Do you have what it takes to be boss?

Sure, we all dream about being in charge, but are your true talents best put to work at the helm, on your own, or as part of a creative team? The answer could lay in this quiz, developed by business strategist Chuck Martin, co-author of *Smarts: Are We Hardwired for Success?*

1. **You get your best ideas when you're:**
   a. In your work space
   b. Talking with friends
   c. In the shower or taking a walk

2. **When you hang a picture, you typically:**
   a. Use a tape measure to be sure it's perfectly centered
   b. Ask someone to hold it while you step back and eyeball it
   c. Put it up where you think it will look right and adjust it afterward, if necessary

3. **You find it easier to remember someone by:**
   a. Name
   b. Where and how you first met
   c. Face

4. **How often do you act on your hunches?**
   a. Rarely
   b. Sometimes
   c. Very often

5. **When you first use a new gadget, you:**
   a. Read the directions carefully
   b. Ask someone to help you figure it out
   c. Just start trying the different features

6. **When you need a quick piece of information from someone, you typically:**
   a. Make a phone call or ask in person
   b. Use e-mail or instant messaging
   c. Save time and look up the answer yourself

7. **How important is it for you to get credit for your work?**
   a. Extremely; when you deserve the credit, you expect it.
   b. Somewhat; only if you put more time and effort into it than others
   c. Not that important; you know what you've accomplished.

Your Score

MOSTLY A'S:

You're a born leader.

Want to find a dream boss? Look in the mirror! You're a great communicator who sees the big picture and knows how to marshal the talent of those around you to achieve a common goal. "Others see your commitment to your work and are inspired by it," says Martin. You have a knack for creating an atmosphere of mutual trust and respect. These are key ingredients for a leader.

MOSTLY B'S:
You're a gifted collaborator.

Creative and naturally social, you come alive when you're part of a group and can tap into that collective energy. "You're a perfect team player because you're not only willing to compromise, but are inspired by brainstorming and sharing ideas," says Martin. Open minded and patient, you thrive on the chance to bounce your ideas off others.

MOSTLY C'S:
You're outstanding on your own.

Quiet and methodical, you work best when given a task and trusted to get it done on your own schedule. You'll never disappoint because you develop your own system for accomplishing your goals and usually go beyond what's expected. "Independent thinkers like you look at familiar situations in a new light and rely on instincts to guide you," says Martin.

21. How do you come up with great ideas?

"Knowing the answer can help you become an even better thinker and master problem-solver," says Larry Ackerman, author of *The Identity Code*.

1. **Your husband wants pizza for dinner; your kids want tacos. You:**
   a. Stop at local take-out places and get both
   b. Flip a coin—the loser's choice will be tomorrow's dinner
   c. Have something everyone likes

2. **When there's a chance of rain in the forecast, you:**
   a. Take your chances and skip the umbrella
   b. Pack a collapsible umbrella in your purse
   c. Wear a raincoat and carry an umbrella

3. **Your jewelry style is:**
   a. Big and bold with lots of fun pieces
   b. Minimal; usually a watch and not much else
   c. Subtle pearls, post earrings, and tennis bracelets

4. **You typically do your laundry:**
   a. When the pile gets too big to be ignored
   b. On the same day every weekend
   c. During the week, whenever it's most convenient

5. **You'd love to own the complete DVD boxed set of:**
   a. *Sex and the City*
   b. *ER*
   c. *Law and Order*

6. **You're most likely to spend your lunch hour:**

a. Eating on the run and doing quick errands

b. Sitting quietly at your desk or in the company lounge or park

c. Out with a few colleagues or a friend

7. **When you buy paper towels you choose by:**

a. Design

b. Brand

c. Price

Your Score

MOSTLY A'S:

Your top problem-solving skill is IMAGINATION.

As a creative problem-solver who thinks outside the box, your greatest gift is the ability to envision the outcome you want and make it happen. "With your confidence and love of a challenge, you're likely to choose the road less traveled when facing a crisis, but that also helps you break new ground and find a successful outcome," says Ackerman.

MOSTLY B'S:

Your top problem-solving skill is LOGIC.

A rigorous thinker who looks at problems earnestly, you feel most comfortable moving in a linear direction—slowly and one step at a time. "You look at all sides of any issue and weigh the pros and cons," says Ackerman. And since you keep a clear perspective during tough times, you don't make snap decisions you'll regret later.

MOSTLY C'S:

Your top problem-solving skill is PROVEN EXPERIENCE.

An avid reader and part-time detective, you put your faith in your own experience or in those in the know, experts and friends who've traveled the same path. "You stay focused on what needs to be done without getting distracted, and you trust the tried-and-true—preferring old-fashioned values to flights of fancy," says Ackerman. Plus, once you find a system that works, you stick with it.

22. What kind of job would make you happiest?

"If you match your personality traits to your job, you'll not only excel—you'll love what you do," says Danielle Perry, spokesperson for www.monster.com, the leading global online career resource. This quiz will help you uncover your strongest traits and the jobs that might best suit you.

1. **When you have a complicated project to tackle you are more likely to:**

   a. Look at the big picture

   b. Focus on one detail at a time

   c. Go where the mood takes you

2. **You communicate in a manner that is best described as:**

   a. Straightforward

   b. Diplomatic

   c. Metaphorical

3. **You tend to:**

   a. Think before you act

   b. Listen before you speak

   c. Think out loud

4. **The inventions you most admire are:**

   a. High tech, such as the latest computer programs

   b. Practical, such as the newest kitchen gadgets

   c. Artistic, such as innovative furniture designs

5. **You usually come to conclusions based primarily on:**

   a. Logic

   b. Personal value

   c. Intuition

6. **Others tend to perceive you as:**

   a. Cool and reserved

   b. Warm and friendly

   c. Quirky

7. **When it comes to spending money, you usually:**

   a. Stick to your budget

   b. Keep an eye on the bottom line—but stay flexible

   c. Spend freely

8. **You are motivated more by:**

   a. Achievement

   b. Helping others

   c. Recognition

9. **When it comes to time, you:**

   a. Are conscious of it—but can get carried away and lose track of it

   b. Are always on time and meet deadlines

   c. Often lose track of it completely

10. **Guests would describe your hostess style as:**

    a. Formal

    b. Casual

    c. Playful

Your Score

MOSTLY A'S:
You are SCIENTIFIC.

As a thinker who is analytical and convinced by logical reasoning, "you'll work best at a job that is structured, ordered, and fairly predictable," says Perry. And since you make decisions based primarily on objective and impersonal criteria and function best in a controlled environment, your most suitable career choices include pharmacist, computer programmer, or laboratory technician.

MOSTLY B'S
You are ADMINISTRATIVE.

Although you keep one eye on the bottom line, you're also a feeler who tends to be sensitive, empathetic, and in constant search for harmony.

"You're naturally expressive and social, so your career option needs to include interaction with other people as well as use of your exceptional organizational skills," says Perry. Good choices are credit counselor, personal shopper, and physician's assistant.

MOSTLY C'S:
You are CREATIVE.

"Visionaries need a job that allows them to use their imagination, see possibilities, tap into intuition—and always face new challenges," says Perry. "Humdrum, detail work and set routine are not for you!" You prefer to keep your options open and are most comfortable adapting. Careers that fit your creative category include entrepreneur, interior decorator, copywriter, and chef.

Millionaire CEOs say they don't consider their jobs ideal and would rather do something more creative. According to a survey, one-third say they would opt for a job as an entertainment event producer—followed by winemaker or chef!

23. Which would you bet on to hit the jackpot?

Who wants to be rich? "We all do—but how we choose to try to attain wealth reveals a bundle about our strengths and priorities," says psychologist Gilda Carle. If you prefer to play:

ROULETTE:
You're sophisticated.

Roulette conjures up glamorous images of James Bond, Monte Carlo, you-in-an-elegant-gown. "If this is your game," says Carle. "You're savvy and grown up." Your sophisticated yet serene personality spills over into other areas of your life: your home is a gracious yet quiet retreat and others marvel at how pulled together and polished you always look. That's why friends often look to you to set the standard, not just for fashion, but for graceful behavior as well.

SLOT MACHINES:
You're passionate.

If you're drawn to the flashing lights, the bells and whistles, and the unmistakable rattle of a big jackpot, "you love drama and spectacle, and you've never lost your childlike enchantment with fun and excitement," says Carle. Always up for a new experience or a last-minute getaway, your passionate, thrill-seeking personality is the spark that enhances all your relationships. Your partner thrives on your spontaneous gestures of love, such as that unexpected extra kiss before he heads out the door, and friends treasure your heartfelt notes and thoughtful gifts. At work, you're filled with a can-do enthusiasm that gets others up and moving—and everyone appreciates the way you inject much-needed fun into their lives.

SCRATCH-OFF TICKETS:
You're a dynamo.

Buy it, scratch, and voilà! There's no need to visit a casino, no reason to mull over what numbers to pick, and no waiting—which is perfect for you. "You're inundated with commitments, family obligations, and ongoing projects," says Carle. "But far from being stressed out, you're always up for a challenge and you enjoy being the one to get the job done." Co-workers rely on you, knowing that whenever there's a project to be tackled you'll be at the head of the pack. But although you're busy, you never forget loved ones. You always make time for them and that's why you appreciate anything that can get you on your way fast—like those scratch-off tickets!

BINGO:
You're popular.

"Bingo is as much about socializing as it is about winning," reveals Carle. The friendship, support, and easy camaraderie you find at your bingo game are more valuable to you than gold. This enjoyment of time spent with pals underscores one of your most important traits: "You're a people person at heart," says Carle. You love to chat and you're loyal to those close to you. New acquaintances are attracted to your outgoing personality and old chums say you're one of their favorite people.

LOTTERY:

You're spiritual.

Do you buy your lottery ticket at the same location every week? Always play your special combination of lucky numbers? Then experts say you're typical of the majority of lottery lovers, who place importance on ritual, tradition, and spirituality. Your sense that one day your numbers will come up shows that "you have strong, unshakable faith," says Carle. The basis of your faith: your family. You can think of no better way to nurture your loved ones than with the same foods, stories, and rituals you loved as a child. Although they may not know it now, you're giving them a valuable gift they'll treasure always!

24. Are you destined for success?

Do you merely dream about being successful, or are you diligently working toward your goal? Take this test and see how you can get ahead!

Part One

1. **You have a chance to study cooking in France with some of Europe's greatest chefs. What do you say?**

   a. "My bags are packed and I'm on my way."

   b. "I'll teach myself, thanks."

   c. "I'd rather treat myself to dinner at a French restaurant."

2. **Choose the "personals" ad you would answer:**

   a. Single male looking for a woman to share the fun times.

   b. Romantic knight wants to share heart and soul with similar woman.

   c. Career-driven single man seeking woman with same goals.

3. **You know that you can handle more work at your job. You:**

   a. Suggest your supervisor give you more responsibilities

   b. Use the extra time to e-mail your friends

   c. Do extra work and hope it's recognized

4. **You need a beauty boost, so you go for:**

   a. A salon trim

   b. A week at a spa to tone your mind and body

   c. A makeover at the best cosmetics counter in town

5. **You've always wanted to write a book. You:**

   a. Tell everyone your idea and take in the feedback

   b. Work on your idea on your own and hold onto it until the time is right

   c. Do research on the Internet on how to get a book published

6. **Which one of these phrases is a bigger part of your vocabulary?**

   a. "I did."

   b. "I'm going to."

   c. "I should have."

7. **Where would you hope to meet the perfect mate?**

   a. At an adult-ed class

   b. Online

   c. At the market or mall

8. **When you have a moment to spare, what are you usually doing?**

   a. Surfing the Net

   b. Daydreaming

   c. Working out your weekly schedule

Part Two

1. **There's so much I want to accomplish!**

   Agree _____ Disagree _____

2. **I don't watch much TV.**

   Agree _____ Disagree _____

3. **One can control fate.**

   Agree _____ Disagree _____

4. **My life has improved in the past seven years.**

   Agree _____ Disagree _____

5. **The best person to depend on is oneself.**

   Agree _____ Disagree _____

Your Score

For Part One, give yourself the following number of points for each answer:

1. a-7, b-5, c-3	5. a-3, b-5, c-7
2. a-3, b-5, c-7	6. a-7, b-5, c-3
3. a-7, b-3, c-5	7. a-7, b-5, c-3
4. a-3, b-7, c-5	8. a-5, b-3, c-7

For Part Two, give yourself 3 points for each statement with which you agreed. Add scores from Parts One and Two.

39 POINTS OR LESS:

Success is within your reach but you haven't stretched far enough to obtain it. Your problem is not laziness—it's fear. In order to fulfill your dreams, you have to risk revealing the real you. This means putting yourself on the line and at the same time, letting go of your insecurity. You're a terrific, smart, witty, warm person. Believe in yourself! You have everything it takes to make all your dreams come true.

40 TO 55 POINTS:

Generally, you feel confident enough to try and reach your goals, especially in your personal life. But when it comes to career moves, you have some blind spots. Perhaps you've spent most of your time as a mom and you don't think you can possibly climb the career ladder. You need to understand that you have a well-spring of life experience to draw upon, and you're plenty capable of finding a job or moving up at work. Make a list of all you've accomplished in your life and you'll see that the key to success is already in hand.

56 POINTS OR MORE:

Brimming with self-confidence and energy, you work to full capacity. First, thank your folks for your positive approach to life. They always said you could do anything if you put your mind to it, and they were right. Whether you're seeking the man of your dreams, working on a creative project, or moving ahead in your career, you do it fearlessly. Just be sure to set aside some time to relax. If you take a breather once in a while, you'll be able to enter every new situation with renewed zeal—and your success rate will be 100 percent!

25. Can you handle power?

Do you delegate authority with kid gloves—or with army boots? Take this test and find out how you'd fare sitting in the director's chair.

Part One

1. **Browsing through the bookstore, you're most likely to reach for a paperback titled:**
   a. *A Lover's Guide to Long-term Lust*
   b. *Recipes for 70 Sensational Sweets and Treats*
   c. *Making Your Way to the Top without Falling off the Ladder of Success*

2. **On average how much time do you spend in bed daily?**
   a. No more than six hours! You're up with the rising sun and bounce out of bed like a bunny rabbit.
   b. You hate to admit it, but about ten hours. You love to cuddle under the covers.
   c. About eight hours. You need time to renew, but you're not a sleep hound.

3. **When you were in grade school, you ran for:**
   a. Cutest girl in school
   b. Class president
   c. Your life! Class bullies were always at your heels.

4. **Your wardrobe consists mainly of:**
   a. Simple suits, silk shirts, and basic pumps
   b. Slinky sheath baby-doll dresses, chunky jewelry, and high-heeled shoes
   c. Sporty sweats, cotton cardigans, and comfy canvas sneakers

5. **The boss left you in charge while on a long vacation. You:**
   a. Seize the opportunity to reprimand a co-worker who deserves it
   b. Take a day off to renew
   c. Keep the shop running in tiptop shape and take pleasure in doing it

6. **Speaking of jobs, your dream profession would be:**
   a. Movie director
   b. Politician
   c. Television host

7. **When an acquaintance confides in you, you are most likely to:**
   a. Take her secret to your grave
   b. Use it for gossip
   c. Let it slip out "accidentally," then try to cover your tracks

8. **Embracing your lover, you whisper in his ear:**
   a. "I'm yours . . ."
   b. "We're one . . ."
   c. "You're mine . . ."

Part Two

1. **Winning isn't everything—but wanting to is!**

   Agree _____ Disagree _____

2. **The best boss is one who absorbs the guff from above and passes down positive feedback.**

   Agree _____ Disagree _____

3. **Procrastination is a waste of time.**

   Agree _____ Disagree _____

4. **I'm bored unless I'm in charge.**

   Agree _____ Disagree _____

5. **Nothing makes me happier than the thrill of a good challenge.**

   Agree _____ Disagree _____

Your Score

For Part One, give yourself the following number of points for each answer:

1. a-2, b-5, c-7	5. a-2, b-5, c-7
2. a-7, b-2, c-5	6. a-5, b-7, c-2
3. a-5, b-7, c-2	7. a-7, b-2, c-5
4. a-7, b-5, c-2	8. a-2, b-5, c-7

For Part Two, give yourself 3 points for each of the statements with which you agreed. Add your scores from Parts One and Two.

39 POINTS OR LESS:

You're out of the running before the race has even begun! Rather than take charge, you choose to shrug your shoulders and let someone else carry the load. Although it's sometimes charming to appear helpless, your friends occasionally find it infuriating. Where's your get-up-and-go? If taking the upper hand is too intimidating, begin slowly by volunteering your opinion. Speak out in a calm, confident voice (try practicing in front of the mirror at home) and listen to yourself. Start mustering your inner resources and, before long, you'll be a dynamo on full blast.

40 TO 55 POINTS:

You've got the strength of an oak along with the endurance to keep going even when the going gets tough. Others look to you for guidance and you have no problem taking the lead. Fair and responsible, you use your power for the betterment of others as well as yourself. You also possess a healthy amount of competitive spirit, which keeps you on the cutting edge. Friends and lovers find your strength admirable because you never use it to manipulate or bully them. Since you're working on all four burners and have confidence and personal magnetism to spare, you're bound for glory.

56 POINTS OR MORE:

You're supercharged for success and you won't let anyone or anything get in your way. Passionate for power, you like to be the person in authority. Unfortunately, you're sometimes a little heavy-handed and just steamroll your way around. Although there's no question you're competent, you might need to take a course in "How to Win Friends and Influence People." Tact is not your strong suit. Adversaries have been known to cower in corners when you want your way. Compromise and compassion are powerful tools; keep those skills in mind while you're soaring to the top.

26. Do you make the most of your time?

Do you make every second count—or do the hours somehow seem to slip right by you? Take this quiz to discover whether you can organize, prioritize, and take care of business—or whether you need help setting goals and sticking to a time-management plan.

1. **Your boss hands you a huge project to organize. You . . .**

   a. Spend a couple of hours complaining before starting to sort things out

   b. Begin the next day when you can start fresh

   c. Get right to work making up color-coded folders

2. **You keep all your CDs and DVDs in:**

   a. Total disarray

   b. Your own personal system

   c. Alphabetical order by artist and title

3. **It's 6:00 pm. The wash is piled up, the house is a total mess, and you can't figure out what to make for dinner. Your solution?**

   a. You give up and turn on the TV. Since you can't do it all, why bother?

   b. You ask your husband to help with the chores.

   c. You flip on the washing machine, call for a pizza, and start cleaning the house.

4. **On Saturday morning, you usually:**

   a. Wake up whenever. You'll just wing the rest of the day.

   b. Sleep until nine, have a leisurely breakfast, then catch up on work you've taken home before starting your household chores.

   c. Get up your usual workweek time, to get through your errands.

5. **It's time to go to the supermarket. You prepare for the trip by:**

   a. Prepare? You just go to the store and get what you think you need.

   b. Checking the kitchen and pantry to get a general idea of what you need.

   c. Making a comprehensive list of everything you need and grab all the coupons you can use.

6. **It's lunch hour and there's an enormous line at the bank. Do you . . .**

   a. Say, "Forget it."

   b. Read the paper while you wait.

   c. Balance your checkbook and revise your to-do list online.

7. **Complete this sentence: "Once I step into a mall I . . ."**

   a. Wander.

   b. Head for my favorite stores but also stop to check out sales.

   c. Get in and out.

Your Score

Give yourself 3 points for each "a" answer, 6 points for every "b"; 9 points for each "c".

21 TO 33 POINTS:
You're the queen of "I'll do it later."

Chances are, your life is more than a little out of control. What you need are some good organizational skills as well as determination. Begin by making a short daily list of things to do. As you complete a task, check it off and congratulate yourself. Soon you'll be able to beat the clock—with time to spare.

34 TO 51 POINTS:
You want to use your time wisely, yet in practice . . .

You schedule your day with the best of intentions, but often you get distracted. Stick to your plans and see projects through to the end. A new sense of accomplishment will spur you on to even greater achievements.

52 POINTS OR MORE:
Time, you realize, is your most valuable commodity.

You make sure every second counts by organizing your work schedule and your life at home. However, a word of caution: remember to stop the clock every once in a while so you have time to reevaluate and appreciate all you've accomplished!

27. Find out how you think on your feet—the secret is hidden in your shoes!

When you're on the job, how does your mind work? The answer may be in your shoes—from how many pairs you own to the styles you love—says Finola Hughes, host of Style Network's *How Do I Look?* Take this quiz to see what kind of thinker you are!

1. **Most of your shoes are:**

   a. Black

   b. Neutrals such as brown, navy, beige, and white

   c. A mix, including vivid colors such as red and lavender

2. **You're more likely to match your shoes to your:**

a. Purse

b. Mood

c. Outfit

3. **You keep your shoes:**

a. Neatly stored on a shoe rack or in a storage bag

b. Under the bed or wherever you last kicked them off

c. In their original boxes

4. **What's the most money you've ever spent on a pair of shoes?**

a. Under $100

b. Not more than $150

c. Over $150

5. **Approximately how many pairs of shoes would you say are in your closet?**

a. A dozen or fewer

b. Between one and two dozen

c. Well over two dozen

7. **Your favorite shoes tend to be:**

a. Flats

b. Sneakers or slip-on athletic-style shoes

c. Heels

YOUR SCORE

MOSTLY A'S:
You're a LOGICAL thinker.

When it comes to decision-making, you prefer researching facts to letting impulses guide you. "That thinking also leads you to choose basic, comfortable shoes that work with any outfit," says Hughes. Your sensible outlook means you stay focused on what matters, and your ability to set goals means you'll go far!

MOSTLY B'S:
You're an EMOTIONAL thinker!

You have no trouble seeing the world through someone else's eyes, and your easygoing nature makes you willing to compromise. "Your shoes, which include many styles, reflect your flexibility," says Hughes. "You choose shoes based on mood, seeking styles that make you feel comfortable and empowered."

MOSTLY C'S:
You're an INTUITIVE thinker.

Free-spirited, impulsive, and instinctual, you make fast decisions and react based on what seems right at the time. You enjoy taking a chance and opt for style over practicality, but you rarely make mistakes! "You're drawn to unique shoes others ignore—until they see them on your trendsetting feet," says Hughes.

Further Reading

INNER LIFE

Brofsky, Howard. *The Art of Listening: Developing Musical Perception*. 5th ed. HarperCollins, 1988.
    http://www.songfacts.com/
    http://www.vtjazz.org/bios/brofsky.html

Carbone, G. G. *How to Make a Fortune with Other People's Junk*. McGraw-Hill, 2005.
    http://ggcarbone.com/
    http://www.keysfleamarket.com/

Cutts, Lynn. *Change One Habit: Change Your Life*. Booksurge, 2005.
    http://www.changeonehabit.com/
    http://www.manageyourmuse.com/index.html

Dossey, Donald. *Holiday Folklore, Phobias and Fun*. Outcomes Unlimited Press, 1992.
    http://www.drdossey.com/holiday_folklore_and_superstitions.htm
    http://www.oldsuperstitions.com/
    http://www.superstitions.ca/

Dugan, Ellen. *Garden Witchery: Magick from the Ground Up*. Llewellyn Publications, 2003.
    http://www.geocities.com/edugan_gardenwitch/

Dunkell, Samuel. *Good-bye Insomnia, Hello Sleep*. Carol Publishing, 1994.
    Sleep Positions: Night Language of the Body. The New American Library, 1978.
        http://www.sleepfoundation.org/
    http://www.sleepnet.com/

Fiore, Neil. *Awaken Your Strongest Self: Break Free of Stress*. American Media International, 2008.
    Awaken Your Strongest Self: Break Free of Stress, Inner Conflict, and Self-Sabotage. Compact disc.
    The Now Habit: Strategic Program for Overcoming Procrastination and Enjoying Guilt-Free Play. Tarcher, 2007.
    http://www.procrastinationhelp.com/people/neil-fiore

Gallagher, Winifred. *House Thinking: A Room-by-Room Look at How We Think*. HarperCollins, 2006.
    The Power of Place: How Our Surroundings Shape Our Thoughts, Emotions, and Actions. Harper Perennial, 2007.
    http://literati.net/Gallagher/

Gediman, Corinne. *Brainfit: 10 Minutes a Day for a Sharper Mind and Memory*. Thomas Nelson, 2005.
    Supercharge Your Memory: More than 100 Exercises to Energize Your Mind. Sterling, 2008.
    http://www.brainfit.net/

Jeffers, Susan. *Embracing Uncertainty: Breakthrough Methods for Achieving Peace of Mind When Facing the Unknown*.
        St. Martins Press, 2003.
    Life Is Hug!: Laughing, Loving and Learning from It All. Jeffers Press, 2005.
    Feel the Fear and Do It Anyway. Ballantine Books, 2006.
    http://www.susanjeffers.com/

Jones, Laurie Beth. *The Four Elements of Success: A Simple Personality Profile that Will Transform Your Team*. Thomas Nelson, 2006.
http://www.lauriebethjones.com/

King, Hans Christian. *Stop Searching and Start Living*. Nightingale Conant Corp, 2004.
Stop Searching and Start Living: Manifesting the Life You Were Born to Live. Audiocassette.
http://www.hansking.com/

Lamberg, Lynne and Michael Smolensky. *Bodyrhythms: Chronobiology and Peak Performance*. ASJA Press, 2000.
The Body Clock: Guide to Better Health. 2nd ed. Holt, 2001.
Crisis Dreaming: Using Your Dreams to Solve Your Problems. ASJA Press, 2001.
http://www.sleephomepages.org/

Mandel, Debbie. *Changing Habits: The Caregiver's Total Workout*. Catholic Book Company, 2005.
Turn on Your Inner Light: Fitness for Body, Mind, and Soul. Busy Bee Group, 2003.
http://www.turnonyourinnerlight.com/

Medved, Denise. *The Bachelor's Tiny Kitchen: A Guide to Cooking and Entertaining*. Tiny Kitchen Publishing, 2003.
The Tiny Kitchen: Cooking and Entertaining. Tiny Kitchen Publishing, 2001.
http://www.thetinykitchen.com/

Messervy, Julie Moir. *The Inward Garden: Creating a Place of Beauty and Meaning*. Little Brown, 1995.
The Magic Land: Designing Your Own Enchanted Garden. MacMillan Publishing Company, 1998.
http://www.juliemoirmesservy.com/

Pieper, Martha Heineman, and William J. Pieper. *Addicted to Unhappiness: Free Yourself from Moods and Behaviors that Undermine Relationships, Work, and the Life You Want*. McGraw-Hill, 2004.
Smart Love. Deutscher Taschenbuch, September 30, 2003.

Steelsmith, Laurie. *Natural Choices for Women's Health: The Secrets of Natural and Chinese Medicine Can Create a Lifetime of Wellness*. Three Rivers Press, 2005.
"Women's Health and Menopause Problems: An Interview with Laurie Steelsmith, ND, Author of Natural Choices for Women's ...Medicine Can Create a Lifetime of Wellness"
http://www.naturalchoicesforwomen.com/

Thorpe, Scott. *How to Think Like Einstein: Simple Ways to Break the Rules and Discover Your Hidden Genius*. Sourcebooks, 2000.
How to Win Like Napoleon. Arch Media, 2007.
http://www.scottthorpe.com/

Treasurer, Bill. *Positively M.A.D.: Making a Difference in Your Organizations, Communities, and the World*. Berrett-Koehler, 2005.
Right Risk: Powerful Principles for Taking Giant Leaps with Your Life. Berrett-Kohler, 2003.
http://www.leadstrat.com/btreasurer.shtml

Trioni, MaryAnn, and Michael Mercer. *Change Your Underwear—Change Your Life: Quick & Easy Ways to Make Your Life Fun, Exciting & Vibrant*. Castle Gate, 1997.
Spontaneous Optimism: Proven Strategies for Health, Prosperity and Happiness. Castle Gate, 1998.

Williams, Redford. *Anger Kills: Strategies for Controlling the Hostility That Can Harm Your Health*. Harper Torch, 1998.
In Control: No More Snapping at Your Family, Sulking at Work, Steaming in the Grocery Line, Seething in Meetings, Stuffing Your Frustration. Rodale, 2007.

RELATIONSHIPS

Bradberry, Travis, et al. *The Emotional Intelligence Quick Book*. Fireside, 2005.
The Personality Code. Putnam, 2007.

Eiseman, Leatrice. *Colors for Your Every Mood*. Capital Books, 2000.
Color: Messages & Meanings: A Pantone Color Resource. Hands Book Press, 2006.
More Alive With Color. Capital Books, 2007.
http://www.colorexpert.com/

Fletcher, Susan. *Parenting in the Smart Zone*. Smart Zone Productions, 2005.
  Working in the Smart Zone Pocket Guide. Smart Zone Productions, 2005.
  http://www.smartzoneexpert.com/

Gallagher, B. J. *Friends Are Everything*. Conari Press, 2005.
  Who Are "They" Anyway? Kaplan Business, 2004.
  Yes Lives in the Land of No. Berret Kohler, 2006.
  http://www.bjgallagher.com/

Gallo, Carmine. *Fire Them Up! 7 Simple Secrets to: Inspire Colleagues, Customers, and Clients; Sell Yourself, Your Vision, and Your Values; Communicate with Charisma and Confidence*. John Wiley & Sons, 2007.
  10 Simple Secrets of the World's Greatest Business Communicators. Sourcebooks, 2006.
  http://www.carminegallo.com

Hartman, Taylor. *The Color Code: A New Way to See Your Relationships, and Life*. Scribner, 2007.
  Color Your Future: Using the Color Code to Strengthen Your Character. Simon & Shuster, 1999.
  The People Code: It's All About Your Innate Motive. Scribner, 2007.
  http://www.thecolorcode.com/
  http://www.hartmancommunications.com/

Hassler, Christine. *20-Something 20-Everything: A Quarter-life Woman's Guide to Balance and Direction*. New World Library, 2008.
  The Twenty Something Manifesto. New World Library, 2008.
  http://www.christinehassler.com/

Hirsch, Alan. *Scentsational Weight Loss: At Last a New Easy Natural Way to Control Your Appetite*. Fireside, 1998.
  What Flavor is Your Personality? Discover Who You Are by Looking at What You Eat. Sourcebooks, 2001.
  What's Your Food Sign?: How to Use Food Cues to Find True Love. Stewart, Tabori and Chang, 2005.
  http://www.smellandtaste.org/

Kemp, Jana. *Moving Out of the Box: Tools for Team Decision Making*. Praeger, 2007.
  No! How One Simple Word can Transform Your Life. AMACOM/American Management Association, 2005.
  http://www.janakemp.com/

Newman, Susan. *Nobody's Baby Now*. Walker & Company, 2003.
  Parenting an Only Child: The Joys and Challenges of Raising Your One and Only. Broadway Books, 2001.
  http://www.susannewmanphd.com/

Oldham, John M. *The New Personality Self-Portrait: Why You Think, Work, Love and Act the Way You Do*. Bantam, 1995.
  http://www.musc.edu/psychiatry/faculty/oldhamj.htm

Puhn, Laurie. *Instant Persuasion: How to Change Your Words to Change Your Life*. Tarcher, 2005.
  http://www.lauriepuhn.com/

CAREER

Ackerman, Larry, and Brian Emerson. *The Identity Code*. Unabridged edition. Blackstone Audiobooks, 2006.
  http://www.theidentitycircle.com/
  http://www.identityisdestiny.com/
  http://www.larryackerman.com/

Barrett, Jayme, and Jonn Coolidge. *Feng Shui Your Life*. Sterling, 2005.
  http://www.jaymebarrett.com/

Canterucci, Jim. *Personal Brilliance: Mastering the Everyday Habits that Create a Lifetime of Success*. AMACOM/American Management Association, 2005.
  http://www.mypersonalbrilliance.com/

Carle, Gilda. *Don't Bet on the Prince! How to Have the Man You Want By Betting on Yourself*. St. Martin's Press, 1999.
  He's Not All That! How to Attract the Good Guys. Collins, 2000.
  http://www.drgilda.com/

Fralix, Patti. *How to Thrive in Spite of Mess, Stress and Less!* Trinity Publishers, 2002.
http://www.fralixgroup.com/

Glickman, Rosaline. *Optimal Thinking: How to Be Your Best Self.* John Wiley & Sons, 2002.
http://www.optimalthinking.com/

Huff, Priscilla. *101 Home-Based Businesses for Women.* Prima Lifestyles, 1998.
Make Your Business Survive and Thrive! 100+ Proven Marketing Methods to Help You Beat the Odds and Build a Successful Small or Home-Based Enterprise. Kindle, 2006.

Jones, Laurie Beth. *The Four Elements of Success: A Simple Personality Profile that Will Transform Your Team.* Thomas Nelson, 2006.
http://www.lauriebethjones.com/

Kassel, Kerul. http://www.stopprocrastinatingnow.com/

Kepcher, Carolyn. *Carolyn 101: Business Lessons from the Apprentice's Straight Shooter.* Fireside, 2005.
www.carolynandco.com/

Martin, Chuck. *Smarts: The Digital Estate: Strategies for Competing and Thriving in a Networked World.* McGraw Hill, 1998.
Are We Hardwired for Success? AMACOM/American Management Association Inc., 2007.

Paul, Marilyn. *It's Hard to Make a Difference When You Can't Find Your Keys: The Seven Step Path to Becoming Truly Organized.* Penguin, 2003.
Why Am I So Disorganized? Sort Out Your Stuff. Piatkus Books, 2007.
http://www.marilynpaul.com/

Pedersen, Sara. *The Busy Mom's Guide to Getting Organized.* Time to Organize, 2006.
Everything You Need to Know About a Career as a Professional Organizer. Time to Organize, 2006.
http://www.time2organize.net/

Pidgeon, Walter P. Jr. *Not-for-Profit CEO Workbook: Practical Steps to Attaining & Retaining the Corner Office.* Wiley, 2006.

Saltz, Gail. *Anatomy of a Secret Life: The Psychology of Living a Lie.* Broadway, 2006.
Becoming Real. Penguin, 2000.
http://www.drgailsaltz.com/

Shapiro, Stephen. *Goal-Free Living: How to Have the Life You Want NOW.* John Wiley & Sons, 2006.
24/7 Innovation: A Blueprint for Surviving and Thriving in the Age of Change. McGraw-Hill, 2007.
http://www.steveshapiro.com/

Spiegel, Jill. *Flirting for Success: The Art of Building Rapport.* Warner, 1995.
Pocket Pep Talk. Goal Getters, 1997.
http://www.flirtnow.com/